ISSUES THAT CONCERN YOU

Dating

Lauri S. Scherer, *Book Editor*

GREENHAVEN PRESS
A part of Gale, Cengage Learning

GALE
CENGAGE Learning·

Detroit • New York • San Francisco • New Haven, Conn • Waterville, Maine • London

Elizabeth Des Chenes, *Director, Content Strategy*
Cynthia Sanner, *Publisher*
Douglas Dentino, *Manager, New Product*

© 2014 Greenhaven Press, a part of Gale, Cengage Learning

WCN: 01-100-101

LIBRARY OF CONGRESS CATALOGING-IN-PUBLICATION DATA

Dating / Lauri S. Scherer, book editor.
    pages cm. -- (Issues that concern you)
 Includes bibliographical references and index.
 Audience: Age 14-18.
 Audience: Grade 9-12.
 ISBN 978-0-7377-6288-4 (hardcover)
 1. Dating (Social customs)--Juvenile literature. 2. Interpersonal relations in adolescence--Juvenile literature. 3. Youth--Sexual behavior--Juvenile literature. 4. Online dating--Juvenile literature. I. Scherer, Lauri S.
 HQ801.D3352 2014
 306.73--dc23
                                                          2013041403

Printed in the United States of America
1 2 3 4 5 6 7 18 17 16 15 14

CONTENTS

From America's high school parking lots to its college dormitories, dating—and the long-term, committed relationships it used to encourage for those in their late teens, twenties, and early thirties—seems to have taken a backseat to hooking up. As more young people delay marriage and other serious commitments, and as women have caught up to men educationally and professionally, hooking up has steadily replaced dating as young people's primary way of interacting romantically. There is enormous debate over whether the emergence of hookup culture is positive or negative, whether it hurts girls or empowers them, and whether it dangerously erodes the fabric of society or is the natural outcome of a society inching closer to gender equality.

On the surface, there appear to be many reasons to bemoan the increased popularity of hooking up. For one, critics say it contributes to increased promiscuity, reduces commitment, deemphasizes nonsexual bonding, and cheapens the physicality that should be reserved for intimate, special relationships. "Under the old model, you dated a few times and, if you really liked the person, you might consider having sex," explains *New York Times* columnist Charles M. Blow. "Under the new model, you hook up a few times and, if you really like the person, you might consider going on a date."[1] Because hooking up normalizes casual sex and often follows alcohol or drug consumption, hooking up may also result in people having sex in vulnerable moments or regrettable ways. In this way it may also contribute to sexual assaults and date rape.

Hooking up has also been criticized for the way in which it might disproportionately hurt girls and young women. Rachel Simmons, an advice columnist for *Teen Vogue*, suggests that hooking up sexualizes girls and leaves them feeling empty, because many tend to value relationships over sexual encounters. Simmons receives hundreds of letters from female readers who lament the circumstances surrounding their various hook-ups and other short-lived sexual encounters. She concludes that hooking up puts girls at a disadvantage because it forces them to give "themselves to guys on guys' terms. They hook up first and ask later. The girls are expected to 'be cool' about not formalizing the relationship. They repress their needs and feelings in order to maintain the connection. And they're letting guys call the shots about when it gets serious."[2]

Simmons and others therefore view hooking up as antifeminist because it puts men in a position of control and power, and despite the fact that such encounters are sold as female empowerment or liberation, they debase and exploit women. "The sexualization of girls and young women has been repackaged as girl power," notes Simmons. "Sexual freedom was supposed to be good for women, but somewhere along the way . . . [it has denied] space for a young woman's feelings and needs."[3] Glenn T. Stanton of the family values group Focus on the Family agrees. "Anyone who believes these girls are empowered, doing exactly what they want to do, when they want to do it, don't know the hearts and minds of most girls," he says. "They want meaningful relationships where their boyfriends commit, taking them seriously and treating them respectfully. It was not young girls who invented the hook-up culture. But they do acquiesce to it."[4]

Meanwhile, others argue that hooking up has positive social benefits. Professor Kathleen A. Bogle, author of the book *Hooking Up: Sex, Dating, and Relationships on Campus*, suggests that hooking up has relieved some of the stigma and social castes created by the pairing imposed by dating culture. In decades in which dating was popular, those with a girlfriend or boyfriend were viewed as cool; those without were not. In contrast, because the hookup culture deemphasizes one-on-one relationships, it removes the negative pressure put upon young people to get a date. "It used to be that if you couldn't get a date, you were a loser," Bogle explains. "Now . . . you just hang out with your friends and hope that something happens."[5]

As for being antifeminist and devaluing women's social currency, *Atlantic* editor and writer Hanna Rosin could not disagree

Whether the emergence of the hookup culture is positive or negative and whether it hurts young women or empowers them is hotly debated.

more. She has called hooking up "an engine of female progress—one being harnessed and driven by women themselves." Rosin looks around and sees a generation of young men and women largely equal to each other, in which women attend college, have careers, and earn money at equal or greater levels than their male counterparts. In part this is because the sexual revolution freed them from the confines of homemaking and child rearing and allowed girls and women to focus on their education and career in ways never before possible. "The whole new landscape of sexual freedom [offers] the ability to delay marriage and have temporary relationships that don't derail education or career," says Rosin. "For college girls these days, an overly serious suitor fills the same role an accidental pregnancy did in the 19th century: a danger to be avoided at all costs, lest it get in the way of a promising future." For Rosin, hooking up is not only *not* antifeminist, it is a marker of how far women have come and can go. As she explains:

> The sexual culture may be more coarse these days, but young women are more than adequately equipped to handle it, because unlike the women in earlier ages, they have more-important things on their minds, such as good grades and internships and job interviews and a financial future of their own. The most patient and thorough research about the hookup culture shows that over the long run, women benefit greatly from living in a world where they can have sexual adventure without commitment or all that much shame, and where they can enter into temporary relationships that don't get in the way of future success.[6]

Still, hookup culture appears to trade in language and behavior that embodies a double standard, including how women who hook up a lot are readily called sluts, whereas men who hook up a lot are viewed as savvy or social. It has also resulted in women, for better or worse, changing their sexual and social behavior, but it has not demanded similar social, sexual, or emotional changes from men. As one college student puts it, "I can tell you first hand, men make out like bandits in this culture. As a male, it's no longer necessary to fulfill roles of commitment. . . . You don't even need much money anymore. It's not often expected of men to have money, and besides, women often have plenty of their own to indulge. . . . Subsequently, all the hard work for guys is gone. We have a broad selection of just about any college age women we want, and few of them need us around the next day."[7]

Issues That Concern You: Dating explores the pros and cons of hookup culture and many other topics related to dating in the modern world. Whether dating websites cultivate quality relationships, whether hookup culture is sexist, and whether dating violence is a serious problem for young people are among the many issues tackled by this collection of engaging and contemporary articles.

Notes

1. Charles M. Blow, "The Demise of Dating," *New York Times*, December 13, 2008. www.nytimes.com/2008/12/13/opinion/13blow.html.
2. Rachel Simmons, "Is Hooking Up Good for Girls?," Rachel Simmons.com, February 25, 2010. www.rachelsimmons.com/2010/02/why-the-hook-up-culture-is-hurting-girls.
3. Simmons, "Is Hooking Up Good for Girls?"
4. Glenn T. Stanton, "Daughters of the Sexual Revolution: Why the Hook-Up Culture Is Sexist," *Christianity Today*, April 25, 2012. www.christianitytoday.com/ct/2012/aprilweb-only/hook-up-culture-sexist.html?paging=off.
5. Quoted in Blow, "The Demise of Dating."
6. Hanna Rosin, "Boys on the Side," *Atlantic*, September 12, 2012. www.theatlantic.com/magazine/archive/2012/09/boys-on-the-side/309062.
7. Uncle_Fred, comment on Rosin, "Boys on the Side."

ONE

The Demise of Dating

Charles M. Blow

> Charles M. Blow is a columnist for the *New York Times*. In the following viewpoint he laments that dating has been replaced with hooking up, which he views as shallow, meaningless physical encounters that at best outdate intimate relationships and at worst increase sexual assaults. He marvels at how young people's personal connections have changed: In the old days, he says, people used to go on dates to determine whether they wanted to get physically intimate. Now, he says, they get physically intimate before they decide whether they want to go on a date. Young people have lost the ability to get to know each other, he fears. Instead, they are forced to hide their feelings and personalities behind sexual encounters, which are usually alcohol fueled. Blow concludes the decline of dating has serious and sad consequences for young people.

The paradigm has shifted. Dating is dated. Hooking up is here to stay.

(For those over 30 years old: hooking up is a casual sexual encounter with no expectation of future emotional commitment. Think of it as a one-night stand with someone you know.)

According to a report released this spring by Child Trends, a Washington research group, there are now more high school seniors saying that they never date than seniors who say that they date frequently. Apparently, it's all about the hookup.

When I first heard about hooking up years ago, I figured that it was a fad that would soon fizzle. I was wrong. It seems to be becoming the norm.

I should point out that just because more young people seem to be hooking up instead of dating doesn't mean that they're having more sex (they've been having less, according to the Centers for Disease Control and Prevention) or having sex with strangers (they're more likely to hook up with a friend, according to a 2006 paper in the *Journal of Adolescent Research*).

"Hooking up" today means a casual sexual encounter with no expectation of future emotional commitment; in other words, a one-night stand.

Hooking Up: Perception Versus Reality

A 2011 study found that students are far more likely to think their peers are hooking up than they actually are. While 90 percent believe their peers are hooking up frequently, only about one-third actually are.

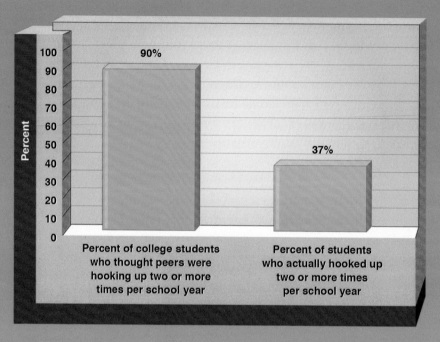

Taken from: A. Holman and A. Sillars. "Talk About 'Hooking Up': The Influence of College Student Social Networks on Nonrelationship Sex." University of Nebraska.

To help me understand this phenomenon, I called Kathleen Bogle, a professor at La Salle University in Philadelphia who has studied hooking up among college students and is the author of the 2008 book, *Hooking Up: Sex, Dating and Relationships on Campus*.

It turns out that everything is the opposite of what I remember. Under the old model, you dated a few times and, if you really liked the person, you might consider having sex. Under the new model, you hook up a few times and, if you really like the person, you might consider going on a date.

I asked her to explain the pros and cons of this strange culture. According to her, the pros are that hooking up emphasizes group friendships over the one-pair model of dating, and, therefore, removes the negative stigma from those who can't get a date. As she put it, "It used to be that if you couldn't get a date, you were a loser." Now, she said, you just hang out with your friends and hope that something happens.

The cons center on the issues of gender inequity. Girls get tired of hooking up because they want it to lead to a relationship (the guys don't), and, as they get older, they start to realize that it's not a good way to find a spouse. Also, there's an increased likelihood of sexual assaults because hooking up is often fueled by alcohol.

That's not good. So why is there an increase in hooking up? According to Professor Bogle, it's: the collapse of advanced planning, lopsided gender ratios on campus, delaying marriage, relaxing values and sheer momentum.

It used to be that "you were trained your whole life to date," said Ms. Bogle. "Now we've lost that ability—the ability to just ask someone out and get to know them."

Now that's sad.

TWO

Reviving a Dating Culture

Meg McDonnell

> In the following article Meg McDonnell argues that young people must revive a culture of dating. Although many of them say they want long-term relationships, very few of them make efforts to this end. Many put their careers before their relationships. Others tend to casually hang out or hook up, which rarely leads to a lasting, meaningful partnership. McDonnell says dates are valuable spaces of time that help two people connect on important and satisfying levels. This is why husbands and wives who go on "date nights" tend to enjoy their marriages and be happier. McDonnell suggests young people should act similarly: They should make room in their lives to pursue meaningful, long-term relationships, which she says are nearly always built on dating. McDonnell is a journalist. Her current project involves marriage trends among young Americans.

"Why is it that so many of these eligible men and women we know who say that marriage is in their future aren't even dating?" My friends and I often muse this. Most of us live in vibrant and fun cities and we aim to surround ourselves with a constant influx of professional, often like-minded, individuals.

Yet my friends and I can count dozens of eligible bachelors and bachelorettes, ourselves often included, who, unless they're very secretive about their dating lives, aren't out on dates very often. And as it turns out, we're not alone in this dating drought.

According to a 2006 Pew Research report, of those singles in America who are eighteen and older and looking for a romantic partner, 49 percent had been on one or no dates in the past month. Twenty-two percent had been on two to four dates. And only a quarter of singles looking for romantic partners had been on five or more dates in the past month. Which raises the question: How do these singles expect to meet their significant other if they're not engaging in the age-old dance of dating?

"[Young adults] are on this trajectory to have great careers by the age of 30," a 23-year-old graduate student told me recently, "but none of us really expect to be single and 30 as well."

"Are you going to play matchmaker at the end of this?" another young woman asked me as I interviewed her about her discontent with the dating culture—or lack thereof—particularly as it related to men expressing interest in her only to never initiate even a first date.

Long gone seems the casual dating environment our parents and grandparents tell us of, when a man asked a woman on a date, not necessarily because he wanted to marry her, but rather because he noticed her. Likewise, a woman was not hesitant to accept such an invitation because, as she saw it, a night on the town was a fun, enjoyable way to see if such a man was a worthy romantic partner. We hear that individuals might have had a handful of such dates during any given week. And that they would forgo other potential significant others when they found one they felt a suitable romantic partner. Today, such casual encounters do happen, but they're so rare that calling them a "casual date" hardly seems appropriate.

Instead, somewhere between hanging out and hooking up, young adults seem to be hoping to find their Mr. or Ms. Right. These vague dating scripts and intentions often leave one or both individuals mildly confused and uncertain as to how to act throughout the entire courting process.

The author laments that today's young people do not experience the style of dating their parents and grandparents did.

Like any goal in life, the quest for romance requires that we keep our eye on the ball and take intentional steps to get there. Happy relationships and marriages aren't born out of thin air, after all.

A report conducted by the National Marriage Project at the University of Virginia summarized that the grassroots initiative "The Date Night Opportunity" for married couples has strengthened a number of areas connected with marital bliss. When couples set aside at least a night a week for fun and enjoyable couple time, as the Date Night Opportunity recommends, married couples are likely to see an increase in communication, novelty or excitement and appreciation, a stronger sense of attraction and a deeper commitment to each other and the relationship.

W. Bradford Wilcox and Jeffery Dew, the writers of the report, summarized that it is unclear if date nights and marital happiness influence one another in a particular way. But one can be certain that date nights and happiness in marriage go together.

What's the lesson for singles looking for romance?

Simply those similar results in dating in marriage can be found in a more consistent dating life for singles. There can be excitement and novelty in dating when the pressure is off to make this rare opportunity work. Additionally, the more an individual dates, the more they'll learn about themselves, the opposite gender, and how to relate to another. Even casual dating, not just hanging out or hooking up, signals that one is serious about their intention to find happy and lasting love.

Dating is just a step on the road to love and marriage, but it's a rather important step, considering it's the start.

THREE

America's Hookup Culture Is Sexist

Glenn T. Stanton

Casual sex and hooking up is sexist against girls, argues Glenn T. Stanton in the following viewpoint. He explains that hooking up has been billed as a form of girl power, a way for girls to feel free and act equal to boys and men. But in reality, he says, girls suffer from sex without commitment. Hooking up leaves them feeling empty and insecure; most do it because they think they are expected to or that it is the only way to get guys' attention. Hooking up is sexist, says Stanton, because girls hurt most from it: They are the ones who must most often deal with sex's consequences, which include getting pregnant, contracting a sexually transmitted disease, and suffering from emotional and psychological trauma. They would much rather have boyfriends, husbands, and meaningful committed relationships. Stanton urges girls to realize that hooking up hurts and limits them, and for all of these reasons he views it as sexist. Stanton is a director at Focus on the Family, a conservative group that advocates traditional and religious family values. He is the author of two books: *Secure Daughters, Confident Sons: How Parents Guide Their Children into Authentic Masculinity and Femininity* and *The Ring Makes All the Difference: The Hidden Consequences of Cohabitation and the Strong Benefits of Marriage*.

The story of girls today is a good news/bad news story. Never before have girls in most of the developed world faced a better shot at a good, successful life in terms of education and fulfilling employment. Starting in 2010, women in the United States are outpacing men in terms of employment. Women are also ruling the board on education, with more ladies earning a bachelor's degree than their male peers. And the *Atlantic* reports that of the 15 top professions to watch in the coming decades, 13 of them are dominated by women. It's not a bad time to be a woman in terms of career development and education. That's the good news.

Loose Sexual Culture Has Hurt Everyone

The bad news is that women are not doing as well in another important area of life: sexuality and relationships. The only winners of the sexual revolution have been the pornographers and other low-life misogynists. It ended up hurting all the rest far more profoundly than anyone ever imagined. Some men might claim it brought plenty of fun, but it aided only the basest part of the male sexual nature which seeks as many women as possible for the least amount of commitment and consideration. The sexual revolution made men neither better nor, as the research consistently shows, happier. However, setting sexuality free from the protective confines of marriage has hurt women more profoundly. And it starts hurting them at very young ages.

This very bad part of the bad news about women is the subject of a new book by two well-respected board-certified ob/gyns [obstetrician gynecologists] who both have long and distinguished careers helping women have sexually healthy lives. Joe McIlhaney and Freda Bush's *Girls Uncovered: New Research on What America's Sexual Culture Does to Young Women* (Moody) is a sharp and well-informed case for why parents, teachers, coaches, and youth leaders need to be mindful of the sexual experimentation among and manipulation of our teen girls. Consider that we give our teenagers more instruction for getting a driver's license or entering college than on how to form healthy, lasting, male-female romantic relationships that lead them into what the overwhelming majority of young people call their number one life goal: a happy, enduring marriage.

Too Much Too Soon

As the father of three teen daughters and one "tween," this book struck a deep chord with me. As a researcher on such matters, it greatly impressed me. I am deeply concerned about the world my girls are increasingly moving into, and I want to make sure that that world treats them with the respect and dignity they very much deserve. Especially the boys. If my wife and I succeed in helping our daughters remain chaste, we will be well in the minority. While only 20 percent of young women answered that oral sex *is* sex (such a question reminds me of the *Saturday Night Live* "Celebrity Jeopardy" skit where Darrell Hammond's Sean Connery is stumped by the category "Colors That End in Urple"), more than 40 percent of 15- to 17-year-olds have had oral sex, while 70 percent of 18-year-olds have done so. And it doesn't get better the older they get. For 20- and 21-year-old women, more than 80 percent report having had both vaginal *and* oral sex. More than 25 percent report having had anal sex. More disturbing, more than 40 percent of early post-teen women report having engaged in oral sex in the last thirty days.

Hooking Up Does Not Empower Girls

Now anyone who believes these girls are empowered, doing exactly what they want to do, when they want to do it, don't know the hearts and minds of most girls. They want meaningful relationships where their boyfriends commit, taking them seriously and treating them respectfully. It was not young girls who invented the hook-up culture. But they do acquiesce to it. While more than 70 percent of girls have sex for the first time with someone they are in a committed relationship with—either "going steady," cohabiting, engaged, or married—it typically doesn't stay that way. A longitudinal survey explains that later sexual activity

More Men than Women Prefer Hooking Up

A study conducted by researchers at James Madison University found college-aged men are much more likely to prefer to casually hook up or date than women.

Men

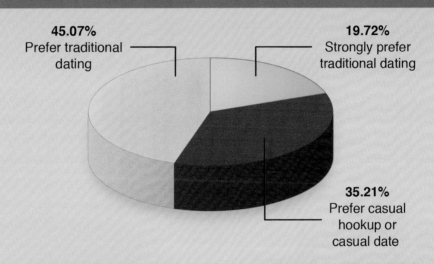

45.07%
Prefer traditional dating

19.72%
Strongly prefer traditional dating

35.21%
Prefer casual hookup or casual date

Women

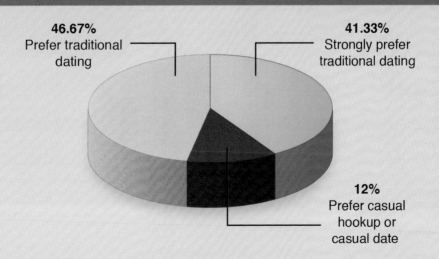

46.67%
Prefer traditional dating

41.33%
Strongly prefer traditional dating

12%
Prefer casual hookup or casual date

Taken from: Carolyn Bradshaw, Arnold S. Khan, and Bryan K. Saville. "To Hook Up or Date: Which Gender Benefits?" *Sex Roles*, vol. 62, no. 9–10, pp. 661–669, 2010.

increasingly morphs into casual hook-ups. This study's authors explained that "the pervasiveness of casual sex was surprising." Among middle-adolescents, 77 percent had moved on to casual sex while 85 percent of late-adolescents had done so.

In a very real sense, early sex in a "committed" relationship is a gateway drug. It usually leads to more dangerous stuff. This is not what girls want. They hook up because they think it's expected of them and because they wrongly believe it's how they can get the guy to pay more attention to them.

Unfortunately, only the guy ends up getting what he's after. And quite often, these are remarkably sharp, beautiful young girls who could be calling the shots in the sexual marketplace, if they

The author says that hooking up leaves young women feeling empty and insecure; most do it because they think they are expected to or because they think it is the only way to get guys' attention.

only realized it. And more often than not, their call would be for dinner, a movie, and a tender goodnight kiss.

The Consequences of Sex Are Sexist

The primary message of *Girls Uncovered* is that sex is sexist: "When it comes to the negative consequences of sexual activity, girls easily get the worst of it." Of course, they are the ones who have to struggle with any resultant pregnancy. But they are also more likely to get a sexually transmitted infection, and the consequences of such infections are typically more severe and longer-lasting in both girls and women. Female physiology doesn't thrive under a diverse sexual resume. Nor does female psychology. Girls also suffer more seriously from depression and self-loathing at the break-up of a sexually active relationship as well as casual hook-ups.

Chastity Empowers Women

Chastity is very good for both young men and women. But it *empowers* women. University of Texas sociologist Mark Regnerus, lead author of *Premarital Sex in America: How Young Americans Meet, Mate, and Think about Marrying* (Oxford University Press, 2011), told me a story of one of his young female students who came to him frustrated that saying "yes" to her suitors' sexual advances didn't seem to help them stick around or increase their genuine interest in her. He recommended she try saying "no" for a few months and see what happens. He followed up with her some months later to see if she took the advice. She told him she had, so Regnerus asked the obvious question: "So?" A sly smile crossed her face, and she said, "I think I'm gonna keep saying no." The feminine mystique is keeping what you have at remarkably high value. Doing otherwise is not empowerment.

FOUR

Society, Not Hookup Culture, Is Sexist

Kate Harding

In the following viewpoint Kate Harding rejects assumptions that hooking up is demeaning to women and that a return to traditional behaviors—such as coy dating and withholding sex—would benefit girls. The problem, in her opinion, is not hooking up. Like all people, girls are a diverse bunch, and thus hooking up is right for some and wrong for others. In addition, women deserve sexual freedom, and she thinks returning to traditional sexual values robs them of autonomy and self-expression. A bigger problem, says Harding, is that society is sexist, since it constantly tells girls to think about what guys want. They are inundated with articles about how to get a guy's attention, what guys love and hate about girls, how to be the perfect girlfriend, and how to perform sexually in ways that men want. Never are they told to think about what *they* want, she says. Harding argues girls should be encouraged to value their wishes and act on their own desires. In doing so, they can more accurately evaluate whether or not hooking up works for them and throw off sexist cultural assumptions that insist women see themselves from men's perspective. Harding is coauthor of the book *Lessons from the Fatosphere: Quit Dieting and Declare a Truce with Your Body*. She writes regularly for the online magazine *Salon*, which originally published this viewpoint.

Is "hook-up culture" a demeaning, destructive thing for girls and young women that would best be remedied by a return to traditional values? Or is it no big deal, the new normal, just something you're too old to understand? That argument never seems to end, despite recent evidence that casual sex does *not*, statistically speaking, ruin young women's lives.

Hooking Up Is Right for Some, Not for Others

Problem is, statistics don't tell the whole story. Rachel J. Simmons, author of *The Curse of the Good Girl* and advice columnist for *Teen Vogue*, says she gets letters all the time from teenage girls who are miserable just hooking up—and for the sake of their emotional health, something's got to give.

"The girls describe themselves as 'kind of' with a guy, 'sort of' seeing him, or 'hanging out' with him," writes Simmons. "The guy may be noncommittal, or worse, in another no-strings relationship. In the meantime, the girls have 'fallen' for him or plead with me for advice on how to make him come around and be a real boyfriend." She worries that these letters "signify a growing trend in girls' sexual lives where they are giving themselves to guys on guys' terms." Noting that sociologist Kathleen A. Bogle found similar stories when she interviewed college-age women for her book *Hooking Up: Sex, Dating and Relationships on Campus*, Simmons suggests that maybe the "old school rules" of dating "made more space for a young woman's feelings and needs" and wonders, "What, and who, are we losing to the new sexual freedom? . . . Is this progress? Or did feminism get really drunk, go home with the wrong person, wake up in a strange bed and gasp, 'Oh, God?'"

OK, that was funny. And I do think Simmons is talking about a real problem here—specifically, "if [girls] get too comfortable deferring to 'kind of' and 'sort of' relationships, when do they learn to act on desire and advocate for themselves sexually?"—but I certainly don't think feminism is the culprit, nor do I even think "hook-up culture" is. I think young women are different—from each other, and often enough from their past and future selves— so it's pointless to keep discussing whether casual sex is All Good or All Bad for them. Here's a thought: Maybe "hooking up" is terrific for some, terrible for others, and somewhere in between for the rest? Sort of like getting married or having children or going into engineering or riding roller coasters or owning a dog or eating sushi—or any other *subjective experience*? Maybe?

Returning to Traditional Values Is Not the Answer

But if we stopped looking at "hook-up culture" as intrinsically good or evil, then what about those young women Simmons and Bogle describe—the ones who feel pressured into accepting arrangements they don't want? Well, here's another thought: What if we focused on teaching girls to "act on desire and advocate for themselves sexually" instead of fretting about an entire generation being ruined by meaningless blow jobs, or longing for a time when the dating "rules" were simpler? (I suppose things *were* significantly less complicated when rape was a "bad date," women were expected to decline sex even when they wanted it, the only acceptable options for pregnant teens were immediate marriage or temporary disappearance, reliable birth control was difficult to come by, ignorance about STIs [sexually transmitted illnesses] was rampant, intimate partner violence was strictly a private matter between two people, etc. Sometimes—I'm just throwing this out there—a little additional complexity might not be a bad thing.)

Teach Girls to Put Themselves First

From where I'm sitting, the problem that needs solving isn't hook-up culture, but the intense pressure on girls and women to focus on getting and keeping a guy, rather than on getting and keeping *whatever they want*. Media aimed at the female of the species from adolescence on up hammers on a few simple messages. 1) If you're not heterosexual—or for some other reason don't see landing a boyfriend as your primary purpose in life—you don't exist. 2) Landing a boyfriend is about understanding What Guys Want and doing whatever it takes to become that. 3) Keeping a boyfriend is about continuing to be What Guys Want, and if your relationship fails, it's probably because you did something Guys Hate.

The author criticizes Seventeen *and other magazines for bombarding young women with information about what guys want.*

Seventeen magazine, for instance, helpfully offers a list of 23 things Guys Hate (sample behaviors: crying, burping, talking about your problems) along with bona fide male answers to burning questions like, "What's your biggest turnoff?" "What's your favorite hairstyle on a girl?" "What's the biggest dealbreaker on a first date?" And, I kid you not, "What's the hottest after-school activity a girl can do?" Once they're a little older, young women can turn to *Glamour* to learn "10 things your man never needs to know," "15 love rules for single women," "10 ways to seduce your man in 10 seconds," "What he really thinks of one-night stands" and of course, "What to do when he's afraid to commit." (Sample advice: "What can you say that won't scare him away? Nothing.")

Enough About What Guys Want

If magazine articles don't provide quite enough detail about how to be What Men Want, then there's the self-help aisle. You could start with something like "Make Every Man Want You: How to Be So Irresistible You'll Barely Keep from Dating Yourself!" Every man, ladies! Not just one or two—*all of them*. Gay, partnered, married, not your type, too young, too old, selfish, addicted, abusive, sociopathic—if you become What Men Want, sexual orientation, personal tastes, geographical boundaries, language barriers and anything else that has henceforth prevented you from attracting *every man* is out the window! You might also check out "Date Like a Man: What Men Know About Dating and Are Afraid You'll Find Out." Because, see, all men know the rules of attraction, but there's no logical reason they'd ever reveal those to potential partners; relationships are intrinsically adversarial. Men *hate* falling in love, making commitments, living with women, having someone who's always there for them, getting to know a partner deeply, and all that other girly [stuff]. They do like sex, though. That's their weakness. And if you find out the Secret Dude Dating Rules they are desperately trying to hide, there is a good chance you could trick them into having sex with you on a permanent basis! Still confused? Then the twice-divorced Steve Harvey is here to help with "Act Like a Lady, Think Like a Man: What Men Really Think About Love, Relationships, Intimacy, and Commitment." If, after all that, you still can't figure out What Guys Want, then I'm not sure what to tell you.

The Problem Is What Girls Are Taught

Except maybe, I don't know, find a guy you like and *ask him* what he wants, on the assumption that he is not, in fact, completely interchangeable with every other man in existence? And tell him what *you* want, recognizing that if your desires and needs aren't going to be met, he is probably not the guy for you? And if that doesn't work out, find *an entirely separate human being* and try again with the talking about what it is you both want? Maybe?

The problem facing these girls writing to Simmons is not that "hook-up culture" has completely destroyed dating, mutual respect, love and commitment. It's that the girls in question don't feel comfortable admitting what *they* want. They've been taught that saying "I want a relationship" or "I'm falling in love with you" will terrify any red-blooded American male—that is so not What Guys Want!—so young women who *are* interested in something more serious are terrified of being alone and completely unwanted if they say so. They've been taught to value male attention so much (if you're hooking up, at least you can be reasonably certain *someone* thinks you're pretty) and their own desires so little, that when they're not getting enough out of a relationship, their first thought is "How can I change so he'll want me more?" instead of, "Well, this isn't working—I'm going to end it and look for a better match." They've been taught that if they're unhappy with a guy, it's probably because they're making Common Dating Mistakes, not because true compatibility is maddeningly uncommon—or because, get this, guys make mistakes, too.

Girls Must Value Their Own Desires

If we stopped telling girls and women how to be What Guys Want (But Would Totally Never Tell You Because Ew, Feelings Are For Girls) and started telling them that what *they* want matters, that every sexual and romantic partnership from a hook-up to a marriage can be fantastic if you *both* want it and miserable if one of you really doesn't, then maybe the ones who want relationships wouldn't get stuck waiting for guys who don't to fall for them. And meanwhile, the ones who enjoy exploring their sexuality more

A 2012 study surveyed more than nineteen thousand college students from twenty-two different colleges. It asked whether students lost respect for men and women who "hook up or have sex with lots of people." It found nearly half lose respect for both men and women.

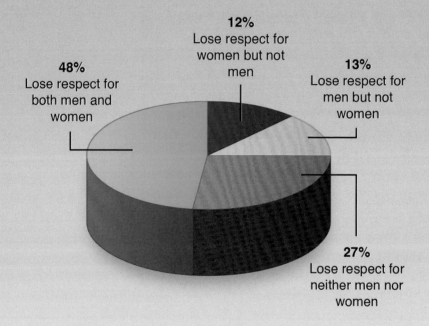

12%
Lose respect for women but not men

13%
Lose respect for men but not women

48%
Lose respect for both men and women

27%
Lose respect for neither men nor women

Taken from: "Study: College Students Lose Respect for Peers Who Hook Up Too Much." American Psychological Association, August 17, 2012.

casually would be free to do so without being slut-shamed, and the ones who don't want guys at all wouldn't be erased from the picture entirely. If we encouraged girls and women to place real value on their own desires, then instead of hand-waving about kids these days, we could trust them to seek out what they want and need, and to end relationships, casual or serious, that are unsatisfying or damaging *to them*, regardless of whether they'd work for anyone else. (While acknowledging, of course, that to some extent, heartbreak and romantic regrets are an inevitable part of growing up.)

The thing is, if only one kind of dating "culture" is acceptable at any given time—whether it's hooking up or old-fashioned courtship—then anyone whose desires don't fit the mold will be left out. But if we teach all kids that there's a wide range of potentially healthy sexual and emotional relationships, and the only real trick (granted, it's a doozy) is finding partners who are enthusiastic about the same things *you* want, then there's room for a lot more people to pursue something personally satisfying at no one else's expense. Doesn't that sound better than trying to turn back the clock?

FIVE

Dating Websites Can Yield Good Relationships

Sean Poulter

> Dating websites lead to love and even marriage, reports
> Sean Poulter in the following viewpoint. He discusses the
> results of a study that found as many as 20 percent of
> people marry the people they meet through such sites. The
> study also revealed the majority of people think it is easier
> to meet people online than at places like clubs, bars, or
> through friends. Such relationships were found to be every
> bit as real as those formed via more traditional channels:
> They feature love, passion, intimacy, and commitment.
> Poulter cites the experience of one couple who married
> after meeting each other online and offers quotes from
> experts and executives in the online dating industry that
> showcase their belief that dating websites are a new way
> to promote old-fashioned love. Poulter is a reporter for the
> *Daily Mail*, a British newspaper that originally published
> this viewpoint.

It has long been seen as a less romantic way of meeting Mr
Right.

But finding love over the internet is a good way of meeting a
marriage partner, research has showed.

Twenty Per Cent of Online Daters Get Married

It found that one in five of those who have used dating sites to find their perfect partner have gone on to marry someone they met over the web.

The study, by consumer group Which?, also revealed that more than half of the 1,504 people questioned had been on a date with someone they met in cyberspace.

Sixty-two per cent agreed that it was easier to meet someone on a dating site than in other ways, such as in a pub or club, or through friends.

At the same time, the under-35s were more likely to know someone who had been on a date or had a long-term relationship with someone they met through online dating.

The author claims that one in five of those who have used online dating sites to find their "perfect" partner have gone on to marry someone they met online.

The survey also found that Match.com and Dating Direct were the most popular dating websites.

A Revolution in the Way People Meet

Jess Ross, editor of which.co.uk, said: 'Online dating is revolutionising the way people meet each other. Switching the computer on could be the first step to success.'

According to industry surveys, more than 22 million people visited dating websites in 2007, and more than two million Britons are signed up to singles sites.

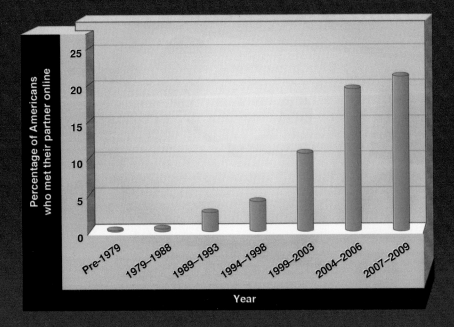

People Can Find Long-Lasting Love Online

By 2009 online dating formed the basis of nearly 25 percent of all long-term relationships.

Taken from: Eli J. Finkel et. al. "Online Dating: A Critical Analysis From the Perspective of Psychological Science." *Psychological Science In the Public Interest*, vol. 13, no. 1, 2012, p. 13.

Previous research has shown that couples who get to know each other via emails are more likely to see each other again after their first date.

Two years ago, a study by Bath University revealed that those who met on dating websites were 94 per cent more likely to see each other after their first meeting than other couples.

The researchers studied relationships formed on online dating website Match.com over a six-month period.

They found that consummate love—described as a balance of passion, intimacy and commitment—was evident at around 12 months into a relationship.

Of the 147 couples who took part in the study, 61 per cent said their relationships had high levels of these three components. The researchers also found that men were more likely to find true love on the internet than women.

Some 67 per cent of men but just 57 per cent of women said they had experienced consummate love with an online partner.

However, women were more likely to experience 'liking' compared to men (9 per cent and 2 per cent respectively), they found.

The Internet Promotes Courtship

Companionate love—a relationship with high levels of intimacy and commitment, but lower levels of passion—was the next most frequently experienced form of love, exhibited by 16 per cent of the study group.

Dr Jeff Gavin, who led the team, said: 'To date, there has been no systematic study of love in the context of relationships formed via online dating sites.

'But with the popularity of online dating, it is imperative we understand the factors that influence satisfaction in relationships formed in this way.'

Charlotte Harper, of Match.com, said: 'We were thrilled to find so many of our former members have found love.

'It supports our belief that the internet does in fact encourage old-fashioned courtship.'

A New Era of Old-Fashioned Love

After failing to find love through the personal ads of his local newspaper, Robert Hammond was keen to give internet dating a go.

The 51-year-old, who works at Leeds University, joined www .parship.com after a series of disastrous dates using other online sites.

He said: 'Parship appealed to me because to join you had to complete an hour's worth of psychometric questions about yourself and interests.

'It means you instantly bypass all those people you are least likely to get along with.

'Martina contacted me shortly after she joined the site. We chatted online for eight weeks before finally meeting up in Berlin, where Martina was living, in May 2007.

'It felt right between us from the start and in October 2007, I proposed at home in Yorkshire. We're getting married on May 30 so, for us, the internet was fantastic.'

Martina Bund, 42, an author, said: 'I had no experience of internet dating so it was luck Robert was the first man I met and the one I'm going to marry.'

SIX

Dating Websites Do Not Yield Good Relationships

Nicole Christopher

> In the following viewpoint Nicole Christopher argues that good relationships are not born from online dating. She tried popular dating sites, thinking they could connect her to people outside her social world. The results were disastrous, however. She met one man who managed to hide his true identity from her for months—it turned out he lied about being married, where he lived, and even about his name. Another person she met online also proved to be a liar. Although they had chemistry over e-mail, in person he turned out to have exaggerated the very qualities Christopher hoped were true. A third attempt at online dating yielded a man who also lied—and lied so much that he did not even remember lying to her months previously. These experiences led Christopher to conclude that meeting people in real life is safer and results in more honest relationships. Christopher is a photographer and writer whose articles have appeared in the *Los Angeles Times*, which originally published this viewpoint.

I am a girl of the new milieu. I have embraced technology with all of its bells and simulated whistles. I am wired to the max—Facebook- and Twitter-connected. My smartphone is plugged in to the outer reaches of the Internet. I purchase shoes, check out real estate and follow various friends on Pinterest. My electronic life has benefited me greatly in all but one area: online dating.

I Gave Online Dating a Shot

At first I drank the Kool-Aid like everyone else. It was easy, and I had a bevy of handsome, well-educated, highly desirable dudes to choose from—or so I thought. Here are a few of my online escapades:

Exhibit A: Leigh, mid-30s, divorced, two kids. He emailed; I emailed in return. I found him refreshing. He wasn't still spewing about his ex; they were actually pleasant to each other and co-parenting their children. I thought that was admirable. He was funny and light in his communications, so I thought, "Why not?" when he asked me out for coffee and cheesecake. He was a gentleman—accommodating, and pleasant in person.

At first our dates were textbook. We met in busy places: lunch at El Cholo, a stroll around the Norton Simon Museum, a fun day of bike riding in Santa Monica. After a few of those day outings, our first dinner was at Sushi Roku. I started to feel comfortable enough to begin dating him on a regular basis.

Then, after a couple of months, I started noticing Leigh would disappear for days at a time. No call. No email. I wasn't too put off at first. I had already met some of his extended family six weeks in, so I wasn't alarmed—until the first night he stood me up and didn't call afterward for days.

Needless to say, after my anger subsided, I forgave him.

We continued, although now I was starting to sense that his stories had holes. After he said he was on his way, he would arrive an hour or so late. He showed up in different cars. I was becoming suspicious.

He stood me up a second time but called six hours later. That prompted me to start digging. I found out that Leigh didn't live

NO E-HARMONY? NO FACEBOOK? HOW DID YOU AND GRANDMA EVER MANAGE TO MEET EACH OTHER?

© Rady Bish/Cagle

where he said he did. He wasn't technically divorced, and "Leigh" was one of several names he used. I didn't know who I was dating. I was done.

I swore off online dating for a while, but after some time, I gave it another shot.

Websites Help People Lie

Exhibit B: David. I was looking for a dance partner, and I was very specific in my profile. David's smile flashed across my screen—tall, handsome and Latino, professing moves that would set the dance floor on fire. I was in.

We agreed to meet at El Floridita restaurant on Vine, where we could get acquainted over dinner and dance to a live salsa band.

When we met at the door, I was caught up in gorgeousness. His smile was warm; his eyes, smoldering. His body was lean and solid. But it was an epic fail! This lovely, handsome man couldn't dance his way out of a paper bag. He had talked such a good game in his emails. But I was embarrassed, disappointed and livid.

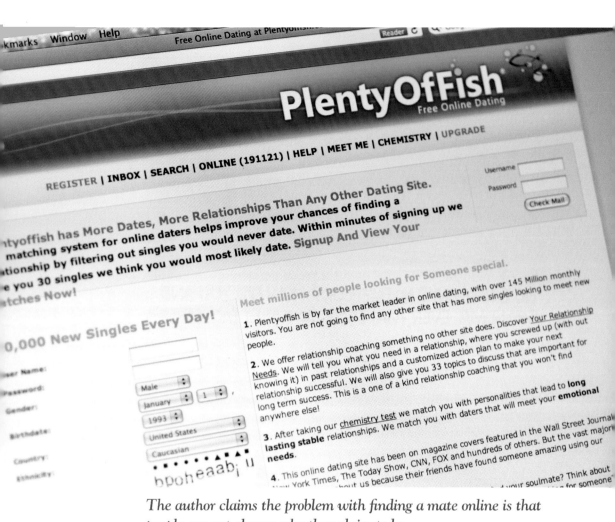

The author claims the problem with finding a mate online is that people are not always who they claim to be.

When I asked him why he'd lied, he spun some story about wanting to go out with me because he thought I was pretty. His talk of dance was to reel me in. "I dance in clubs. Isn't that enough?" he asked. But I couldn't bear to stick around to see what else he was going to lie about.

The Freaks Come Out

Exhibit C: Ron, who didn't even make it to coffee-date status. Ron and I had met on dating site A (which shall remain nameless). We shared a few emails. He told me he was caring for his Down syndrome brother—who had seen my photo and urged him to contact me. Ron wrote a few cute stories about his sibling, and they tugged at my heartstrings.

The more I began to ask questions about his brother and his illness, the more Ron began insisting that we meet. He started to sound rather desperate and needy. Then, in one email, he mentioned that he had taught his brother about sex by watching pornography. Which was, to put it mildly, a red flag. I ceased communication with Ron immediately.

A year later, trying my luck on another dating site, I received a brand-new email from Ron (and his brother). He gave me the exact same story about how his Down syndrome brother encouraged him to email me. He didn't remember me at all, typing out the same old tired lies as before. So I emailed him back and asked how he and his brother were enjoying their adventures in porn.

I never heard from Ron again.

Real-Life Interactions Are More Honest than Online Interactions

There it is: exhibits A, B and C. That's why I'm not interested in what the World Wide Web has in store for my dating life now. I absolutely refuse to allow my love life to enter into unharmonious union with online dating sites. I'd rather take my chances on real-life interactions. Online dating is one brave new world that this technology queen is going to shun.

SEVEN

The Scientific Flaws of Online Dating Sites

Eli J. Finkel and Susan Sprecher

Online dating has serious flaws and weaknesses, argue Eli J. Finkel and Susan Sprecher in the following viewpoint. They conducted an extended study on how online dating sites work. They found that people who use online dating sites are not good at recognizing compatible qualities in online profiles and thus make poor decisions about potential mates. Even more importantly, the study found serious problems with the complicated formulas used by such sites to match people—the formulas do only a slightly better job at matching people than random contact in real life. Dating websites do not reveal the math behind their formulas, which Finkel and Sprecher regard as deceptive and suspicious. They conclude that dating websites use unscientific methods and shoddy math to match people with no greater accuracy than in-person encounters afford. People should save their money and concentrate on meeting other people in real life, they suggest. Along with Paul W. Eastwick, Benjamin R. Karney, and Harry T. Reis, Finkel and Sprecher are the authors of "Online Dating: A Critical Analysis from the Perspective of Psychological Science," which was published in the January 2012 issue of the journal *Psychological Science in the Public Interest*.

Every day, millions of single adults, worldwide, visit an online dating site. Many are lucky, finding life-long love or at least some exciting escapades. Others are not so lucky. The industry— eHarmony, Match, OkCupid, and a thousand other online dating sites—wants singles and the general public to believe that seeking a partner through their site is not just an alternative way to traditional venues for finding a partner, but a superior way. Is it?

With our colleagues Paul Eastwick, Benjamin Karney, and Harry Reis, we recently published a book-length article in the journal *Psychological Science in the Public Interest* that examines this question and evaluates online dating from a scientific perspective. One of our conclusions is that the advent and popularity of online dating are terrific developments for singles, especially insofar as they allow singles to meet potential partners they otherwise wouldn't have met. We also conclude, however, that online dating is not better than conventional offline dating in most respects, and that it is worse in some respects.

Beginning with online dating's strengths: As the stigma of dating online has diminished over the past 15 years, increasing numbers of singles have met romantic partners online. Indeed, in the U.S., about 1 in 5 new relationships begins online. Of course, many of the people in these relationships would have met somebody offline, but some would still be single and searching. Indeed, the people who are most likely to benefit from online dating are precisely those who would find it difficult to meet others through more conventional methods, such as at work, through a hobby, or through a friend.

For example, online dating is especially helpful for people who have recently moved to a new city and lack an established friendship network, who possess a minority sexual orientation, or who are sufficiently committed to other activities, such as work or childrearing, that they can't find the time to attend events with other singles.

It's these strengths that make the online dating industry's weaknesses so disappointing. We'll focus on two of the major weaknesses here: the overdependence on profile browsing and the overheated emphasis on "matching algorithms."

Ever since Match.com launched in 1995, the industry has been built around profile browsing. Singles browse profiles when considering whether to join a given site, when considering whom to contact on the site, when turning back to the site after a bad date, and so forth. Always, always, it's the profile.

What's the problem with that, you might ask? Sure, profile browsing is imperfect, but can't singles get a pretty good sense of whether they'd be compatible with a potential partner based on that person's profile? The answer is simple: No, they cannot.

A series of studies spearheaded by our co-author Paul Eastwick has shown that people lack insight regarding which characteristics in a potential partner will inspire or undermine their attraction to him or her. . . . As such, singles think they're making sensible decisions about who's compatible with them when they're browsing profiles, but they can't get an accurate sense of their romantic compatibility until they've met the person face-to-face (or perhaps via webcam; the jury is still out on richer forms of computer-mediated communication). Consequently, it's unlikely that singles will make better decisions if they browse profiles for 20 hours rather than 20 minutes.

The straightforward solution to this problem is for online dating sites to provide singles with the profiles of only a handful of potential partners rather than the hundreds or thousands of profiles that many sites provide. But how should dating sites limit the pool?

Here we arrive at the second major weakness of online dating: the available evidence suggests that the mathematical algorithms at matching sites are negligibly better than matching people at random (within basic demographic constraints, such as age, gender, and education). Ever since eHarmony.com, the first algorithm-based matching site, launched in 2000, sites such as Chemistry.com, PerfectMatch.com, GenePartner.com, and FindYourFaceMate.com have claimed that they have developed a sophisticated matching algorithm that can find singles a uniquely compatible mate.

These claims are not supported by any credible evidence. In our article, we extensively reviewed the procedures such sites use to build their algorithms, the (meager and unconvincing) evidence they have presented in support of their algorithm's accuracy, and whether the principles underlying the algorithms are sensible. To be sure, the exact details of the algorithm cannot be evaluated because the dating sites have not yet allowed their claims to be vetted by the scientific community (eHarmony, for example, likes to talk about its "secret sauce"), but much information relevant

A series of studies has shown that people looking for a mate on dating sites do not recognize compatible characteristics in a potential partner and thus often make poor choices. The authors also question the validity of dating sites' algorithms for matching people.

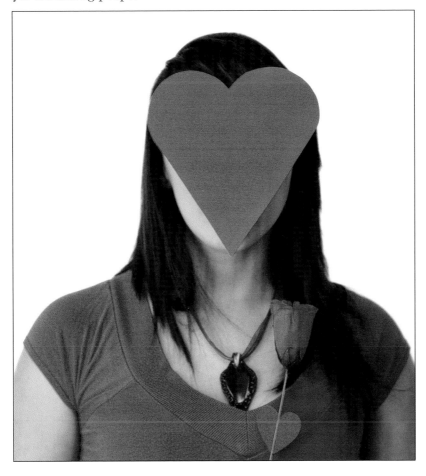

to the algorithms is in the public domain, even if the algorithms themselves are not.

From a scientific perspective, there are two problems with matching sites' claims. The first is that those very sites that tout their scientific bona fides have failed to provide a shred of evidence that would convince anybody with scientific training. The second is that the weight of the scientific evidence suggests that the principles underlying current mathematical matching algorithms—similarity and complementarity—cannot achieve any notable level of success in fostering long-term romantic compatibility.

It is not difficult to convince people unfamiliar with the scientific literature that a given person will, all else equal, be happier in a long-term relationship with a partner who is similar rather than dissimilar to them in terms of personality and values. Nor is it difficult to convince such people that opposites attract in certain crucial ways.

The problem is that relationship scientists have been investigating links between similarity, "complementarity" (opposite qualities), and marital well-being for the better part of a century, and little evidence supports the view that either of these principles—at least when assessed by characteristics that can be measured in surveys—predicts marital well-being. Indeed, a major meta-analytic review of the literature by Matthew Montoya and colleagues in 2008 demonstrates that the principles have virtually no impact on relationship quality. Similarly, a 23,000-person study by Portia Dyrenforth and colleagues in 2010 demonstrates that such principles account for approximately 0.5 percent of person-to-person differences in relationship well-being.

To be sure, relationship scientists have discovered a great deal about what makes some relationships more successful than others. For example, such scholars frequently videotape couples while the two partners discuss certain topics in their marriage, such as a recent conflict or important personal goals. Such scholars also frequently examine the impact of life circumstances, such as unemployment stress, infertility problems, a cancer diagnosis, or an attractive co-worker. Scientists can use such information about people's interpersonal dynamics or their life circumstances to predict their long-term relationship well-being.

But algorithmic-matching sites exclude all such information from the algorithm because the only information those sites collect is based on individuals who have never encountered their potential partners (making it impossible to know how two possible partners interact) and who provide very little information relevant to their future life stresses (employment stability, drug abuse history, and the like).

So the question is this: Can online dating sites predict long-term relationship success based exclusively on information provided by individuals—without accounting for how two people interact or what their likely future life stressors will be? Well, if the question is whether such sites can determine which people are likely to be poor partners for almost anybody, then the answer is probably yes.

Indeed, it appears that eHarmony excludes certain people from their dating pool, leaving money on the table in the process, presumably because the algorithm concludes that such individuals are poor relationship material. Given the impressive state of research linking personality to relationship success, it is plausible that sites can develop an algorithm that successfully omits such individuals from the dating pool. As long as you're not one of the omitted people, that is a worthwhile service.

But it is not the service that algorithmic-matching sites tend to tout about themselves. Rather, they claim that they can use their algorithm to find somebody uniquely compatible with you—more compatible with you than with other members of your sex. Based on the evidence available to date, there is no evidence in support of such claims and plenty of reason to be skeptical of them.

For millennia, people seeking to make a buck have claimed that they have unlocked the secrets of romantic compatibility, but none of them ever mustered compelling evidence in support of their claims. Unfortunately, that conclusion is equally true of algorithmic-matching sites.

Without doubt, in the months and years to come, the major sites and their advisors will generate reports that claim to provide

Types of US Online Dating Sites and Their Distinctive Features

There are dozens of different dating sites. Some match people by mathematical formula; others use technology that finds potential dates in a person's immediate vicinity.

Row	Type of Site	Distinctive Feature	Example Sites
1	General self-selection sites	Users browse profiles of a wide range of partners	Match, PlentyOfFish, OkCupid
2	Niche self-selection sites	Users browse profiles of partners from a specific population	JDate, Gay, SugarDaddie
3	Family/friend participation sites	Users' family/friends can use the site to play matchmaker for them	Kizmeet, Heartbroker
4	Video-dating sites	Users interact with partners via webcam	SpeedDate, Video dating, WooMe
5	Virtual-dating sites	Users create an avatar and go on virtual dates in an online setting	OmniDate, Weopia, VirtualDateSpace
6	Matching sites using self-reports	Sites use algorithms to create matches based on users' self-report data	eHarmony, Chemistry, PerfectMatch
7	Matching sites not using self-reports	Sites use algorithms to create matches based on non-self-report data	GenePartner, ScientificMatch, FindYourFaceMate
8	Smartphone apps	GPS-enabled apps inform users of partners in the vicinity	Zoosk, Badoo, Grindr

Taken from: Eli J. Finkel et al. "Online Dating: A Critical Analysis from the Perspective of Psychological Science." *Psychological Science in the Public Interest*, vol. 13, no. 1, 2012, p. 8.

evidence that the site-generated couples are happier and more stable than couples that met in another way. Maybe someday there will be a scientific report—with sufficient detail about a site's algorithm-based matching and vetted through the best scientific peer process—that will provide scientific evidence that dating sites' matching algorithms provide a superior way of finding a mate than simply selecting from a random pool of potential partners. For now, we can only conclude that finding a partner online is fundamentally different from meeting a partner in conventional offline venues, with some major advantages, but also some exasperating disadvantages.

EIGHT

In Wake of Southfield Motel Murder, Seven Notable Cases of Online Dating Gone Wrong

Aaron Foley

Aaron Foley is a reporter for MLive.com, a news website that serves the state of Michigan. In the following viewpoint he argues that online dating—like other online activity—can be very dangerous. People often misrepresent themselves online, he says, lying about their identity and intent so they can take advantage of others. Sometimes people create fake dating profiles to meet other people, whom they rob, cheat, beat up, rape, or even murder. Foley lists several instances in which criminals used dating websites to find victims. He warns that even when people act sensibly—which includes not giving out their personal information, not revealing their address or location, and not meeting people without a trusted friend or family member's knowledge—they have fallen victim to schemes and scams. He warns people to exercise the utmost caution when using online dating sites.

Almost anyone with a working Internet connection knows the dangers and risks of meeting someone online. Still, it's hard to ignore the sparkling ads for sites like eHarmony.com, or the easy thrills of sites like Craigslist.

And we've heard the rules ad nauseum about navigating the tricky waters of online dating and meeting: Don't give out personal information. Have a friend on standby ready to come to the rescue. Don't get too serious. Don't say anything—or respond to anything—that could get you in trouble. And, as always, buyer beware.

But the murder of a Metro Detroit man is the latest in a string of online dating gone wrong. Is it easy to fall into a trap even when playing by the rules? Possibly. Here are seven online dating cases with varying circumstances, and varying degrees of tragedy.

1. In Southfield last weekend, 35-year-old West Bloomfield resident Venkata Cattamanchi arranged a date with 23-year-old Jessica Ermatinger of Canton, police say. After meeting at a restaurant, the pair traveled to a motel, where Cattamanchi was allegedly robbed and murdered by three men waiting there. Ermatinger and the three men were charged with murder and robbery.

2. In March, a Ferndale man was beaten and robbed by a man he met online and an accomplice. The two men are accused of tying him up, beating him with a hammer and a handgun, taking his ATM card and withdrawing money from his bank account. One of the men was dressed as a woman.

3. In December, a St. Clair Shores man set up a date with a woman he met through MySpace. While the pair were at dinner, the woman's accomplice cleaned out the man's apartment—after she allegedly tipped him off via text message. They were charged with stealing $11,000 worth of the guy's stuff; she took a plea deal, he was sent to prison.

And outside of Metro Detroit . . .

4. In 2006, 28-year-old Michael Sandy of New York was killed after arranging a date through a gay chatroom. Sandy arranged to meet a man in a park, but instead was met with a group of men who robbed and beat him. While attempting to escape, Sandy

was chased into traffic and hit by a car. Three men were sent to prison for his murder, while a fourth took a plea deal in exchange for testifying against them.

5. Also in New York, a New York woman who posted a Craigslist ad offering masseuse services was killed in a Boston hotel by a man who answered her ad. 28-year-old Julissa Brisman is thought to be the third victim of 24-year-old Philip Markoff,

Accused Craigslist killer Phillip H. Markoff (right) is arraigned in Boston, Massachusetts, for the murder of masseuse Julissa Brisman in April 2009. Markoff used the popular site to find his victims.

her alleged killer. Markoff is allegedly linked to the murders of two other women who posted ads on Craigslist. He is scheduled to go to trial next year.

6. Pretty much every episode of Chris Hansen's "To Catch a Predator."

7. In 2006, two teen girls in Florida set up a fake MySpace profile to lure men into robbing them. A 14-year-old and a 15-year-old girl met a man at an apartment who was "just lookin' for some fun," but robbed him at gunpoint. When police found them with another teen male accomplice, they retrieved two loaded handguns.

NINE

Teen Dating Violence Is a Serious Problem

American Psychological Association

In the following viewpoint the American Psychological Association asks psychologist Sherry L. Hamby questions about teen dating violence. Hamby reports that teen dating violence is a real and serious problem—while other forms of violence are on the decline, teen dating violence rates are holding steady. In fact, such violence affects as many as one in thirteen teens, she says. Teen dating violence is characterized by extreme jealousy, monitoring and controlling physical and emotional abuse, and other behaviors. Teen dating victims are also more likely to suffer from other problems such as cyberbullying, stalking, social isolation, anxiety, and depression. Hamby and the American Psychological Association urge teens, their parents, and other parties to look for signs of teen dating violence and intervene where they can.

*I*n February, romance is typically associated with Valentine's Day. But for some teens, a dating partner can prove to be abusive rather than affectionate. Some teens become violent or abusive to exert power and control over a dating partner. February is national Teen Dating Violence Awareness Month, an opportunity to provide teens, their *parents, educators and friends information and resources to recognize and prevent teen dating violence.*

Psychologist and APA [American Psychological Association] member Sherry L. Hamby, PhD, is a research associate professor at Sewanee, the University of the South, and a research associate with the University of New Hampshire Crimes against Children Research Center. . . .

APA recently asked Dr. Hamby the following questions:

Jealousy and Control Inform Dating Violence

APA: Why do some teens become violent toward their dates? Are there signs a teen should look for in a prospective date before deciding to go out?

Dr. Hamby: Teen dating violence doesn't just spring from nowhere. Both teens who use violence and those who are vulnerable to being victimized have typically experienced previous victimizations, harsh parenting and other adversities. Some of the most dangerous youth are those who expect their dates to meet all of their emotional and social needs. Jealousy—especially jealousy that is way out of proportion to how long a couple has been dating or how serious their relationship is—is a big warning sign. So are controlling and monitoring behaviors. If you have to send your boyfriend a picture from your phone to prove that you are really at your grandmother's house, that's a problem.

Youth who turn to violence to solve other problems are also at increased risk of perpetrating teen dating violence.

Teen Dating Violence Is a Real Problem

Has teen dating violence increased in recent years, and if so, why? Are there usually more incidents near or on Valentine's Day?

Our data show the rate of teen dating violence is holding fairly steady, unlike some forms of violence which are dropping. Dating violence affects approximately one in 13 youth. Also, there is the problem not only of the persistence of physical teen dating violence but the emergence of new forms of abuse, such as cyberbullying and cyberstalking.

Victims of teen dating violence are three to four times more likely than other teens to be cyberbullied.

Valentine's Day and other holidays or special occasions present increased risk largely due to increased consumption of alcohol. Data show that physical violence is more than three times as likely on days that alcohol is consumed compared to days with no drinking. This pattern also holds for psychological aggression, especially for males, who are more than seven times as likely to be psychologically aggressive on days when they drink, while females are about one-and-a-half times more likely. Valentine's Day can also increase vulnerability because research has shown that for some teens it can be a day associated with intercourse, including first sexual intercourse.

The Link to Social Media

Does the research show any links between teen dating violence and today's increased use of social media?

Yes, our new study coming out in *Psychology of Violence* provides the first nationally representative data showing a strong association between teen dating violence and cyberbullying. Victims of teen dating violence are three to four times more likely to be cyberbullied as other teens. These aren't all boyfriends and girlfriends abusing each other online and in person. It reflects a pervasive vulnerability for all teens that is probably due to parents, teachers and other adults failing to prioritize the safety of teens in their lives.

What to Look For

What are some of the behavioral signs of a teen who is a victim of teen dating violence?

Parents and other concerned adults can watch for a dramatic decline in contact with other friends. It is natural that a boyfriend and girlfriend will want to spend time together, and this will often take up some of their free time that previously might have been spent with other peers. Still, it is important to maintain nondating friendships and it is worrisome if time with friends falls to near zero or they seem anxious about making plans that don't include their partner. Of course, classic signs of psychological distress, such as symptoms of anxiety or depression, are associated with teen dating violence and numerous other problems and should be investigated.

What to Do

What should parents do if they suspect their child is a victim of dating violence? What can teens do if they are a victim or if they know someone who is a victim?

There are many steps that parents and other bystanders can take, starting with simply expressing concern and offering to be a safe, nonblaming person to talk to about relationships. Parents are

Teens and Dating Violence

In 2012 the Robert Wood Johnson Foundation surveyed more than 1,400 seventh grade students on their experiences with various types of dating violence. More than 1 in 3 students reported being a victim of psychological dating violence, and more than 1 in 6 said they had experienced physical dating violence.

33.2%	15%	31%
report being a victim of psychological dating violence in previous 6 months	report being a victim of physical dating violence in previous 6 months	report being a victim of electronic dating violence in previous 6 months

Taken from: Robert Wood Johnson Foundation, March 2012.

important role models for teens (whether it seems like it or not) and also need to make sure their own relationships are respectful and egalitarian. Speaking up when you see someone being treated badly is also a way to help create community norms that promote healthy relationships. Finally, all parents should know about resources in their area and online. No matter where you live in the United States, teens, parents or anyone else can call the National Domestic Violence Hotline at 1-800-799-SAFE or loveisrespect at 1-866-331-9474, text "loveis" to 77054.

TEN

Teen Dating Violence Has Been Exaggerated

Benjamin Radford

Benjamin Radford is the managing editor of *Skeptical Inquirer*, a science magazine that critically evaluates news, studies, and other materials. In the following viewpoint he argues the problem of teen dating violence is overblown. He discusses one study that claimed to find widespread evidence of dating violence among teens. But the study, according to Radford, used poorly worded questions that exaggerate the extent of the problem. For example, rather than asking teens if they had ever been in an abusive relationship, it asked them if they *knew* anyone who was in an abusive relationship. Radford points out that even if 100 percent of those polled say yes, they could all be referring to the same one person they know. Radford says studies that examine teen violence must be better constructed so as not to incite panic on the issue or give the impression the problem is more widespread than it is.

A recent study made headlines across the country: The "Tween and Teen Dating Violence and Abuse Study" was commissioned by Liz Claiborne and the National Teen Dating Abuse Helpline. Among the headlines: 62 percent of 11- to 14-year-olds know someone in an abusive dating relationship, and one in five of those age 13 to 14 knows someone who has been struck in anger by a dating partner.

A Hidden Epidemic or an Invented One?

According to one reporter from a Las Vegas newspaper, "The image of the innocence of youth was shattered by the new study," which "found shocking horrors in teen dating."

In an effort to show just how shocking and unexpected the findings were—even to teens themselves—the reporter interviewed two teens. One high schooler, Ryan Sniezyk, said that he doesn't think that any of his friends are being abused. "I don't know anything about that," he said. "Maybe they are keeping it from me." Another young man agreed, saying that his experience didn't reflect the new study's findings.

The dating violence may be a hidden epidemic, or there may be another reason that the statistics are shocking and the teens don't know anything about it: They aren't accurate.

Misleading Data About Teen Dating Violence

Parents may want to remove their fingers from the panic button and take a closer look at the study. Some of the most alarming statistics are misleading.

First, a quick quiz: Let's say you read a statistic from a study that says 75 percent of students at Harvard say they know someone who has cheated on a test. What does that mean? Does that mean that three-quarters of Harvard students are cheaters? Many people will read it that way, but they are wrong. In an extreme hypothetical explanation for how wrong this could be, it's possible that only one student at Harvard cheated, but everyone knew about him.

The teen dating study contained many questions asking the respondent if they knew other people who experienced certain events. For example, question 11 is: "Do you know anyone among your friends and people your age who have been called names, put down, or insulted?"

The author believes that the statistics published in the National Teen Dating Abuse Helpline report on teen violence are inaccurate and show such violence to be more prevalent than it really is.

That's a simple, clear question that does not yield a simple, clear meaning because the answer tells us very little about the prevalence of abusive behavior. It doesn't take into account multiple reporting of the same incident among survey respondents. For example, let's say there's a fight at a high school and someone gets stabbed. If you later take a survey of students at the school and ask them if they know or heard about anyone who was stabbed, hundreds of people will say yes. But that doesn't mean that hundreds of people were stabbed, it just means that all of the people asked had heard about the one person who was attacked.

Many of the teen dating study's questions suffered exactly this problem.

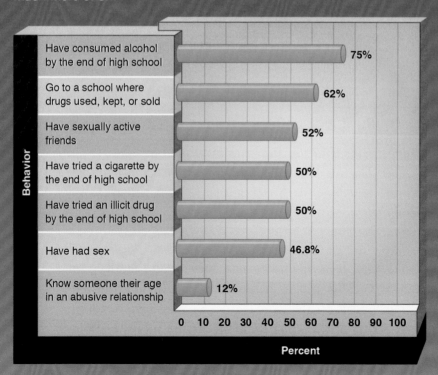

Keeping Teen Dating Violence in Perspective

Although teen dating violence is worrisome, it occurs much less frequently than other problems or high-risk behaviors among teens. High school students report engaging in the following behaviors much more often:

Behavior	Percent
Have consumed alcohol by the end of high school	75%
Go to a school where drugs used, kept, or sold	62%
Have sexually active friends	52%
Have tried a cigarette by the end of high school	50%
Have tried an illicit drug by the end of high school	50%
Have had sex	46.8%
Know someone their age in an abusive relationship	12%

Taken from: Julie Ray. "Adolescents Not Invulnerable to Abusive Relationships." Gallup, May 24, 2005: SADD (Students Against Destructive Decisions), 2006.

Poorly Conducted Studies Serve No One

What is needed are valid numbers on the number of people *actually* being abused, not percentages of people who have *heard about* others' abuse. There's also the problem of definitions. The study includes being called names or being put down as abuse. By this definition, if anyone you have been involved with has ever put you down or criticized you, you were in an abusive relationship. With such a broad definition, the high abuse rates found are hardly "shocking."

Statistics don't speak for themselves, they must be interpreted with caution. If you don't know what questions were asked, how they were phrased, or don't understand what the answers mean, the numbers are meaningless. There may indeed be "shocking horrors" in teen dating, but these particular statistics do not reflect them. Teen dating violence and domestic abuse are serious issues, and deserve both credible research methods and good journalism.

ELEVEN

Date Rape on College Campuses Is a Serious Problem

Tina deVaron

Date rape is a serious problem on college campuses, argues Tina deVaron in the following viewpoint. She reports that 25 percent of all female college students are sexually assaulted, usually by their fellow classmates. DeVaron has personal experience with this topic: She was raped as a college student, and the experience continues to haunt her. Date rape is particularly problematic on college campuses because of alcohol abuse, fraternity culture, and a male-dominated culture that still believes "no means yes," she says. Women also fear their stories will not be believed, since their rapists are their fellow classmates, dorm members, and teammates, many of whom take advantage of situations in which appropriate conduct is already blurry. She urges men and women on campuses everywhere to recognize that date rape is a real and serious problem that must be curbed. DeVaron is a singer and pianist who performs in the New York City area.

The recent "She Roars" conference at Princeton celebrated 42 years of coeducation and featured such powerhouse alumnae as [Supreme Court] Justice Sonia Sotomayor, former eBay CEO Meg Whitman, and Teach for America founder Wendy Kopp. When I entered Princeton in 1973, the university had been

Tina deVaron, "At Colleges Plagued with Date Rape, Why 'No' Still Means 'Yes'," *Christian Science Monitor*, June 28, 2011. This article first appeared in The Christian Science Monitor (www .CSMonitor.com).

coed for four years. Now, it was hosting a celebration of women's empowerment, unveiling a landmark study on undergraduate women's leadership.

Mimicking Rape Is Not Funny

On the conference's opening night, a female a cappella group, the Princeton Tigerlilies, gave a concert. The girls sang prettily, dressed in short black frocks and high pumps.

Then the group's all male a cappella counterpart, the Nassoons, performed. For the song "ShamaLama," they serenaded one of the Tigerlilies onstage, with choreography: In rhythm, they pantomimed unzipping their flies, and bluntly thrust their pelvises forward at the lone young woman on stage. Sixteen guys, one girl. The guys smirked, the girl smiled meekly.

I am an ex-director of a collegiate a cappella group. As are my husband and both of our sons. We're steeped in the traditions and humor. But this was worse than tacky. Women around me were agape with disbelief.

Should we have been surprised, with Yale being sued for its frat boys chanting "No means yes," and headlines on alleged sexually predatory behavior dominating the news (think Dominique Strauss-Kahn[1])? Despite decades of women's "empowerment," male sexual prerogative is alive and well in our society, and among these Princeton undergrads.

Remembering a Rainy Night in 1973

My She Roars schedule showed no events addressing this kind of hostile environment or date rape—and only a glancing reference to sexual assault in the "Undergraduate Women and Leadership" report.

I began feeling angry. Because of the way my own life had changed at Princeton during freshman year. On a rainy night,

1. The former director of the International Monetary Fund who allegedly sexually assaulted a hotel maid.

College Campuses and Rape

The Rape, Abuse & Incest National Network (RAINN) reports that rape on college campuses is not reported to authorities as often as it occurs. Using statistics from the US Department of Justice and the National Crime Victimization Survey, RAINN has made the following conclusions about rape on college campuses.

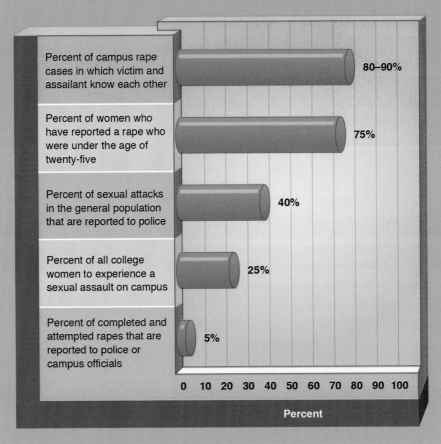

Percent of campus rape cases in which victim and assailant know each other — 80–90%

Percent of women who have reported a rape who were under the age of twenty-five — 75%

Percent of sexual attacks in the general population that are reported to police — 40%

Percent of all college women to experience a sexual assault on campus — 25%

Percent of completed and attempted rapes that are reported to police or campus officials — 5%

Percent

Taken from: Rape, Abuse & Incest National Network (RAINN), 2009.

whose events I'd suppressed for years until hearing a report about date rape on NPR [National Public Radio] brought it back.

Following a big exam, my resident advisor (RA) treated his rugby friends and me to a beer at a neighborhood roadhouse. After we returned to the dorm and said our goodnights, there was a knock at my door. The rugby team captain asked if he could sleep on my roommate's vacant bed, since it would be such a rainy walk up campus.

I still don't know why I let him in. I was not drunk; I remember every minute of the next hour. I said no, he said yes. I struggled; he was the rugby player. When he had finished raping me, he went back to his dorm in the rain. I remember him calling the next day to "see how I was." I remember hearing people laughing in the background.

He was the friend of my RA, someone I respected. It didn't make sense. I told no one. I stayed in my nightgown the whole next day.

For years I thought that by letting the guy in, I was somehow complicit in the crime.

I Did Not Consent

I wonder about the climate for Princeton women now, where girls smile prettily while sixteen men pantomime what is essentially gang rape in front of an audience of middle-aged women, many of them moms.

Sexual conquest for a nineteen-year-old man is one step on the ladder to success. Not so for the nineteen-year-old girl who did not consent.

When the memories of my incident surfaced, I called my pastor. She had had a similar experience as an undergrad. How many others are keeping this hidden?

I am lucky, married to a man who respects and loves me, and the mother of two sons who are self-aware gentlemen. Why not simply be grateful for this wonderful conference at my alma mater, filled with brilliant women and old friends? Why write about this now?

Our Culture Has Not Changed

Because I still carry the events of 37 years ago with me, as will many woman who have been raped. And because there is a girl reading this now who will be starting at Cornell in the fall, or

Penn State, or Miami, who will be entering an environment largely unchanged from the Princeton campus I walked onto nearly four decades ago.

It's a culture where "no still means yes." It's a culture where male sexual dominance (and violence) underlies daily interac-

The author believes that date rape on college campuses persists because many schools still have a male-dominated "no means yes" culture.

tions, frat parties, and even a cappella concerts. Skeptics might protest, "They were only having harmless fun. Those guys aren't rapists." But it's precisely this kind of attitude of sexual conquest that entitles men to rape women. And there's nothing harmless about that.

Campuses Entitle Men to Rape

The date rape statistics speak for themselves. One in four women will be sexually assaulted on a college campus. Between 15 and 30 percent of college women have been victims of acquaintance rape at some point in their lives. And these aren't violations at the hands of strangers on the street.

According to the National Victims Center, 84 percent of women know their assailant. And 57 percent of rapes occur on a date. For women victims ages 18 to 29, two-thirds know their attacker. And more than 60 percent of rapes occur in residences.

That's the reality we're sending our bright college women into. In context, the antics of those college a cappella boys aren't the stuff of innocent comedy. Those moves are representative of a larger culture that accepts and desensitizes us to sexual violence against women.

This Serious Problem Must Be Addressed

I keep asking myself: Why was there nothing in Princeton's She Roars conference that addressed this? College campuses can no longer afford to be complicit in this culture. Women—*and* men— need to take a stand to change the language, the behaviors, the relationships, the clubs, and the institutions that allow it.

The benefit will be a wiser, more open, more equal society in general.

And perhaps the men's a cappella performance at the next She Roars conference will not be quite so tone-deaf.

TWELVE

Are One in Five College Women Sexually Assaulted? The Vice President Buys into the Campus-Rape Lie

Heather Mac Donald

The problem of date rape on college campuses has been exaggerated, argues Heather Mac Donald in the following viewpoint. If campus rape statistics were true, she argues, parents would send their daughters off to college with personal bodyguards and other defensive tools. They do not, however, because the problem has been astronomically exaggerated, she says. While some claim that rape victims do not report the experience out of fear, Mac Donald says a more likely explanation for the silence is that rape is simply not happening. She points to several flawed studies that rely on loose or false definitions of campus rape to exaggerate the prevalence of the problem. In some instances, for example, women who were classified as rape victims actually said they had not been raped. Mac Donald says college women tend to believe they have been raped after failing to remember a drunken night of sex. She says this is not real rape, but a case of someone stupidly putting themselves in a situation with sexual consequences. She urges college women to not get so drunk that they are unable to control their sexual encounters and also asks college and government officials to stop selling rape as an invisible crisis. Mac Donald is a fellow at the Manhattan Institute and a contributing editor for *City Journal*, where this viewpoint was originally published.

Imagine that there were a "terrible and alarming trend" of sexual violence on college campuses against female students. Imagine that 20 percent of college women were victims of rape or attempted rape—a rate of sexual assault astronomically higher than anything seen in America's most violent cities (in Detroit, for example, there were 36.8 rapes per 100,000 inhabitants in 2009, a rate of 0.037 percent). If 18-year-old girls were in fact walking into such a grotesque maelstrom of sexual violence when they first picked up their dormitory room key, parents and students alike would have demanded a radical restructuring of college life years ago. There would have been a huge surge in all-girls colleges to protect female students from these outrageous levels of sexual violence; those colleges that did still admit boys and girls together would have been forced to prove to worried parents that the boys they were admitting were not rapists—perhaps allowing parents to interview these aspiring monks before they were accepted. Just to be on the safe side, administrators would provide round-the-clock protection for their female students.

Instead, over the last decade or so, the proportion of female students in co-ed colleges has skyrocketed, so that there are now more girls than boys in most of the nation's co-ed schools. Parents relentlessly push their daughters into the most prestigious schools they can get into; competition among female students to enroll in co-ed colleges has never been higher. None of those girls demand bodyguards as a condition of acceptance; instead, their parents feel fortunate to cough up tens of thousands of dollars a year to keep their daughters on campus, where they are free to boogie through as many drunken frat parties as they can before passing out from overinhalation of Kahlua and Crème.

And yet, according to Vice President Joe Biden, the Justice Department, and the Education Department's Office of Civil Rights, college is in fact a nightmarish gauntlet of sexual violence and abuse. "There is a terrible and alarming trend in the country of sexual violence [on campuses]," Russlynn H. Ali, assistant secretary of education, told the *New York Times*. Ali's Office of Civil Rights is investigating Yale for maintaining a "sexually hostile environment." Somehow that sexually hostile environment did not discourage thousands of the country's most academically gifted females from beating down the doors to get in; the acceptance rate at Yale this year was 7.35 percent, the lowest rate ever.

The White House claims that one in five female students has been victims of sexual assault or attempted sexual assault while at college. Such bogus statistics have been the mainstay of campus-rape-epidemic propaganda for years. They are generated by a variety of clever techniques, but the most important is this: The survey-taker, rather than the female respondent, decides whether the latter has been raped or not. When you ask the girls directly whether they view themselves as victims of rape, the answer overwhelmingly comes in: No.

Biden has just announced more college red tape on the laughable ground that schools ignore sexual violence. In fact, virtually every campus has a robust sexual-violence bureaucracy which sits idle, waiting for the shell-shocked casualties of rape to crawl through their doors. The victims never come—because they don't exist. But pressure from the feds will undoubtedly give those lonely college rape counselors further clout to push for increased funding, even as schools cut their German and Latin programs for lack of money. Meanwhile, the parallel campus sex bureaucracy—the Sex Toy Dispensary and Good Vibe Advice Office—continues to do record business, while the occasional professor even offers live XXX shows.

Here is the reality on campuses, which the free-love baby-boomer college deans and provosts will never acknowledge: The sexual revolution and the disappearance of adult moral authority on campus have resulted in a booze-filled sexual free-for-all, in which testosterone-charged boys act boorishly, and the girls compete to match them in reckless promiscuity. (Only disrespect for "diversity" causes the deans and provosts to exercise any moral

The author claims the best advice for someone who wants to avoid being date raped is to avoid excessive alcohol intake.

The Role of Alcohol in Campus Rape

Brown University reports that as many as 70 percent of college students admit to having sex as the result of being drunk, or to having sex they would not have engaged in if sober. Many such encounters are not remembered by students. Some argue that these encounters are not really rape, but rather the result of alcohol abuse.

Percent of students involved in acquaintance rape who admit to using alcohol or drugs at the time of the incident

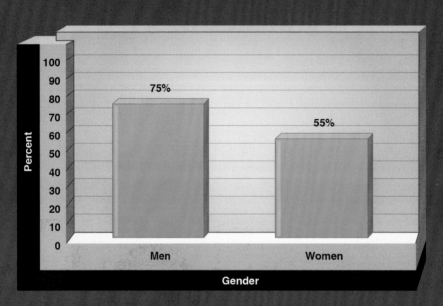

Taken from: American Institute for Preventative Medicare, 2012.

oversight over their students.) Yes, there are plenty of drunken hook-ups that result in the proverbial "roll and scream": "You roll over the next morning so horrified at what you find next to you that you scream," as Laura Sessions Stepp reported in *Unhooked*. A small percentage of those next-day regretters view themselves as having been raped; most think that they acted stupidly and irresponsibly.

There are a few, simple antidotes to the alleged campus-rape crisis: Don't drink yourself blotto. Don't get into bed with one of your fellow drunken revelers. Keep your clothes on. If every girl practiced those elementary rules, poor Ms. Ali might be out of a well-paying government job.

THIRTEEN

Student-Teacher Dating Should Be Illegal

Hannah Dreier

In the following viewpoint Hannah Dreier reports on efforts to make student-teacher dating illegal. Supporters of such efforts argue that such relationships are always inappropriate, even when the student is of legal age. For one, teachers hold power over their students—young people cannot credibly claim the relationship is equal, because teachers are their authority figures. Secondly, even though an eighteen-year-old is legally allowed to have sex with someone older, it is impossible to prove whether a physical relationship began earlier than that. In the case of student-teacher relationships, teachers may ready their students for a sexual relationship before they turn eighteen, which is predatory and abusive, even though technically not against the law. To avoid these gray areas, a law outlawing such relationships entirely could protect students. Dreier is a reporter for the Associated Press, a national news service.

A 41-year-old high school teacher exchanges a flood of text messages with his student, then leaves his wife and three children to date her. The couple then goes on national TV, saying their relationship didn't become physical until she turned 18.

In California, there's nothing illegal about what they did.

Inappropriate Relationships Should Be Illegal

Now, a lawmaker is hoping to change that with a bill rolled out Tuesday [in March 2012] that would make such relationships a felony, even if the student is 18, and strip school employees of their pensions and retiree health care if they are convicted.

To prevent teachers from "grooming" students for relationships when they become adults, the bill would also criminalize seductive communication, including sexual text messages.

"Our hope is that that will be a pretty strong and painful deterrent and will cause someone to think twice before starting an inappropriate, unethical relationship with a student," said Republican Assemblywoman Kristin Olsen, the bill's sponsor.

Teachers would get back whatever contributions they had made to the public pension system.

California is considering banning student-teacher relationships, such as the one between eighteen-year-old Jordan Powers and her former teacher, James Hooker, forty-one (pictured).

Affairs Should Be Illegal Regardless of Age

If the bill is successful,[1] California would join 23 other states in banning student-teacher affairs regardless of age, according to Olsen. These include Texas, North Carolina, Ohio, Connecticut and Kansas. In some states, such affairs are a felony.

Olsen is from Modesto, a city about 75 miles south of Sacramento where teacher James Hooker and student Jordan Powers struck up their relationship at Enochs High School. Powers has dropped out, but Hooker's 17-year-old daughter still attends.

The announcement of their relationship made national headlines. In interviews for the *Dr. Phil* show and ABC's *Good Morning America*, the couple can be seen holding hands and exchanging smiles.

Powers' mother, Tammie, confronted the couple on "Dr. Phil" and accused Hooker of brainwashing her daughter. Web commenters have also poured on criticism.

To Prevent an Abuse of Power

The couple maintains that, while they met when Jordan was 14, their relationship did not become physical until she was of age, meaning that it is permissible under current laws. California's age of consent is 18.

Hooker and Powers could not be reached for comment Tuesday [March 27, 2012]. Powers moved out of her house, and Hooker's phone is disconnected.

The elder Powers has been touring national talk shows raising the alarm about such relationships.

At news conference with Olsen to announce the bill, Powers said she welcomes the media attention that has surrounded her daughter's case and vowed to get similar legislation passed in every state.

"I had no legal recourse whatsoever with an 18 year old, and I believe that the teacher pursued her," she said. "So this will be a preventative measure."

Law enforcement officials are investigating the case.

1. On April 24, 2012, the California Assembly's Committee on Public Safety rejected the bill.

Nearly Half of All States Have Laws Against Student-Teacher Dating

As of 2012 twenty-three states (including Texas, North Carolina, Ohio, Connecticut, and Kansas) have prohibited dating between eighteen-year-old students and their teachers.

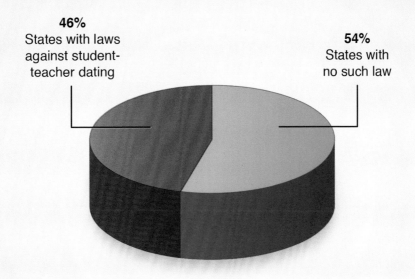

46%
States with laws against student-teacher dating

54%
States with no such law

Taken from: "California Bill Would Punish Student-Teacher Dating." Associated Press, March 27, 2012.

Older Teachers May "Groom" Their Victims

Affairs between teachers and of-age students are frowned upon in California but not illegal. The issue is left to policies set by individual school districts.

In the state's largest district, Los Angeles Unified, the code of conduct for teachers prohibits any communication between teachers and students that is not school-related, according to district spokeswoman Gayle Pollard-Terry.

If the relationship did not turn physical until recently, Stanislaus County Sheriff Adam Christianson said, there is little they can do.

Christianson said his time in the high-tech crimes unit showed him the importance of cracking down on inappropriate communication between children and adults.

"We know for a fact that pedophiles are predators, and they groom their victims long before they victimize them," he said.

There's no way to know how often these teacher-student relationships develop.

Since her daughter's story broke, Powers said she received more than 5,000 emails from all over the country, many from parents worried that their own children may be in a similar situation.

Olsen's bill is one of several measures Republicans are proposing to make it easier for school districts to fire and punish educators who engage in inappropriate behavior.

One of the measures would strip convicted felons of their state pensions, a bill inspired by the recent case of a former Los Angeles teacher charged with 23 counts of lewd acts against children.

Olsen, who has three children of her own, said teachers need to face harsher punishments when they violate the community's trust by seducing their students.

"We think that when we send our kids to school, these are safe and secure positive learning environments," she said.

FOURTEEN

Student-Teacher Dating Should Not Be Illegal

Rebecca Kling

It should not be against the law for eighteen-year-old students to date their teachers, argues Rebecca Kling in the following viewpoint. She acknowledges that teachers hold a special authority over their students. But in the law's eyes, eighteen-year-olds are adults—they have legal authority over themselves, and this includes having sex with whomever they want. Kling thinks what is legal outside of school should be legal in school, too. Furthermore, she thinks teachers should be treated like other professionals, who are entitled to a private life outside of their workplace. For all of these reasons, she thinks that student-teacher relationships should not be against the law as long as a student is eighteen years old. Kling is an artist and educator.

As a teacher who works with children in middle and high school, I understand the relationships and intimacy which can develop between teachers and students. I've worked with some of my students for over a decade, seen them grow into confident young adults, and watched them go off to college. Some stay in touch, and some cross my mind from time to time as I wonder what they're up to today. I hope I do a good job steering them in through tumultuous childhoods and teenage years, and aim to leave them better people than they were when [they] first came to work with me. I'm also a theatre instructor who generally sees my students once a week, so I have limited impact, but I can still dream of making a difference; I know how powerfully my teachers—even those I saw infrequently—affected my development into an adult.

Teachers Must Be Allowed Lives Outside of School

All these thoughts crossed my mind as I heard that the Arkansas Supreme Court had struck down a law 4–3 which forbade teachers from engaging in sexual activity with students who were under the age of 21. I feel pretty strongly that behavior outside of one's employment shouldn't be a factor in how they're viewed as an employee. I hate the stories of teachers who are fired for having drunk pictures show up on Facebook, and I think drug screening for applicants is inherently unjust and offensive. For me, as a transgender lesbian, it's all too easy to imagine my "personal life" being viewed as offensive or unacceptable when it comes to my professional life. Indeed, I was fired from a teaching position for being trans, which has nothing to do with my ability to teach a class.

So, my gut reaction is that, yes, if the relationship (in this case between an 18 year old student and her 36 year old teacher) is legal outside of school, it should be legal in school.

Age Is Arbitrary

Upon further reflection, however, teacher-student relationships create an inherent power dynamic. Sexual activity between minors and adults is forbidden (at least in part) because there's an inherent imbalance of power. It is impossible for a child to maturely provide consent to an adult in the way two adults (or, arguably, two children) are able to do.

But these lines are arbitrary. No one thinks that a flip is switched at exactly 16 that makes people able to drive, or at

The author believes that if an eighteen-year-old's relationship with an older person is legal in the state it should be legal in school.

exactly 18 that makes people able to vote or smoke, or at exactly 21 that makes people able to drink. Societies create arbitrary lines in the hope that—for the majority of the population—those lines will do a pretty good job of keeping the "too young" on one side and the "old enough" on the other. Yet teacher/student is a more clearcut relationship. You stop being a student when you *graduate*, not when you reach a specific age. So should a teacher/student sexual relationship—illegal and generally agreed to be a bad thing at 17 years, 11 months, and 30 days—suddenly be acceptable at 18?

From the three dissenting justices: "For the majority to say that such authority vanishes when a student turns 18 ignores the realities of the student-teacher relationship," Brown wrote. "I cannot agree that a teacher has a right protected by our constitution to engage in sexual contact with a student."

Treat Legal Adults like Adults

Many students turn 18 while in their senior year of high school (myself included) they're judged "too young" in one way—they're still in high school, a place for children—but "old enough" for lots of things as far as legality is concerned. I remember realizing, after I turned 18, that I no longer needed to take permission slips home for my parents to sign. When we went scuba diving in the school pool (which was awesome, by the way) I took the form, signed it myself and handed it right back. I was legally allowed to make that decision, even though I was still a student as far as the school was concerned; I had to obey the period bells, get to class on time, and so on.

And yet I keep returning to the fact that we judge people—rightly or wrongly—to be adults at 18. There isn't a case-by-case test or a subjective panel or a medical diagnosis. On one's 18th birthday, they're an adult. Which, to me, means they should be allowed to sleep with their teacher. Even if it makes me uncomfortable. Even if I question the inherent power dynamic of such a relationship. Even if the school gets really worried about potential liability. They're an adult. Treat them like one.

FIFTEEN

The Case for Cohabitation

Hannah Seligson

> In the following viewpoint Hannah Seligson argues that couples should live together before they get married. She says living together before marriage does not increase a couple's chance of divorce, nor does it amount to accepting a relationship out of convenience, rather than love. Most couples decide to live together because they truly want to—very few move in together to save money. Living together before marriage is also a good way to see if people are compatible for marriage, she says. Society is critical of this arrangement because some people remain very conservative, but in reality, cohabitation is a good fit for many young couples. She suggests people take a more enlightened view of living together outside of marriage and realize it can have many benefits. Seligson is a contributor to the *Daily Beast*, which publishes left-leaning news and commentary.

It's springtime, and love is in the air—which means that lots of 20somethings are packing up their belongings and embarking on a romantic rite of passage that has become *de rigueur*: moving in with their significant other.

Yet if Sunday's viral *New York Times* op-ed, "The Downside of Cohabitation Before Marriage," is to be believed, this now beyond-mainstream part of the modern dating dancer—living together before marriage—should be met with great caution, if not downright avoided. Here's why, according to the author of the piece, Meg Jay, a Charlottesville, Va., psychologist who specializes in treating young adults.

"Couples who cohabit before marriage (and especially before an engagement or an otherwise clear commitment) tend to be less satisfied with their marriages—and more likely to divorce— than couples who do not. These negative outcomes are called the cohabitation effect."

Jay spotlights the oft-cited argument that cohabitation is a casual arrangement that just happens—in the lexicon of researchers, "sliding, not deciding." And once two people shack up, it's harder for them to disentangle, leaving many young people with the double-whammy of being stuck in a living arrangement that was born out of convenience (and that can turn awkward fast), and one that leads to a tepid level of commitment and a doomed marriage. Or so the theory goes. But cohabitation researchers see the outcomes a little differently.

"Some of the most recent studies are finding no effect on the likelihood of divorce, even along racial and class lines," says Pam Smock, director of the Population Studies Center at the University of Michigan, who has been researching cohabitation for two decades.

"Cohabitation may actually be keeping divorce rates steady by weeding out couples who would have been more likely to get divorced had they not lived together and realized they weren't compatible. A lot of these cohabitation relationships do breakup," Smock points out.

And a breakup, as we all know, is a lot better than a divorce.

Sharon Sassler, a professor of policy analysis and management at Cornell University who has extensively studied cohabiters, agrees that there is a lot of mythology surrounding cohabitation—and says statistics that correlate living together with higher divorce rates are outdated.

Cohabitation Is on the Rise

Since 1982 cohabitation rates for women have nearly quadrupled, with more than 11 percent of fifteen- to forty-four-year-olds reporting living with their partner outside of marriage.

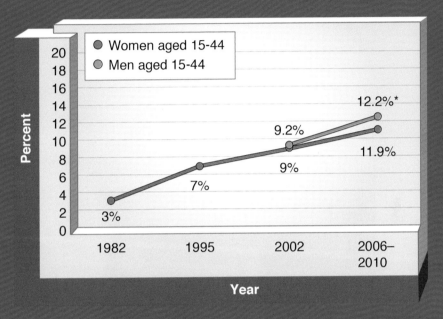

*The study only looked at data for men beginning in 2002.

Taken from: C.E. Copen, et al. "First Marriages in the United States: Data from the 2006–20120 National Survey of Family Growth." National Health Statistics Reports, no. 49, Centers for Disease Control and Prevention, March 22, 2012.

More recent studies, Sassler says, signal an alarm bell only for a select group: serial cohabiters. "People who live with multiple partners have higher divorce rates. If you've only lived with the person you are going to marry, you have no greater chance of getting divorced than a couple who hasn't lived together," Sassler explains.

What about the insidious tumble effect—or in the parlance of the demo, "Your lease is up, my lease is up, so, sure, let's move in together?"

This phenomenon also needs a disclaimer, says Amanda Miller, a professor of sociology at the University of Central Oklahoma who has researched the mechanics of cohabitation. "You really have to take class into account," Miller says. "In the research Sharon Sassler and I conducted, we found that middle-class couples were far more likely to have the luxury to decide to move in together rather than sliding into it."

For some couples, living together before marriage is a good way to see whether they are compatible for marriage.

Like with marriage, cohabitation's storyline is very much driven by class. Miller and Sassler found that lower-income participants felt they had to move in together because someone's roommate moved out and they couldn't afford to live alone, whereas middle-income participants more often reported making a conscious choice to live together.

As for cohabitation's effect on getting married, Miller says the middle-income couples aren't tying the knot because someone needs health insurance or they've already lived together for seven or eight years. "For them, marriage is a deliberate and well-thought out choice. We found, at least in our sample, that the middle-class men love the women and wanted to be married."

So if cohabitation isn't necessarily a divorce sentence for a relationship—or a procrastination tool for marrying—why do we still see fairly regular critiques of cohabitation? To start, young people's romantic, and by extension sexual, choices have a long history of being stigmatized. Look no further than the outrage over premarital sex, even after the advent of birth control.

Today, with the exception of pockets of religious communities and Rick Santorum, we've mostly gone sex-positive as a nation—there's now "sex week" on a large smattering of college campuses, and condoms, while occasionally controversial, are not hard to find at the vast majority of health centers. In other words, we have more or less embraced the reality that young people have sex before they get married, so they might as well be doing it safely.

Yet cohabitation seems to have replaced premarital sex as the axe to grind among everyone from social conservatives to psychologists. Given that 70 to 90 percent of young people will live together before they get married, though, it's a pretty shortsighted view to the issue.

Of course, not everyone takes the wagging-finger approach. In New Zealand, for example, to reflect the large numbers of heterosexual people living together outside of the typical bonds of marriage, the country progressed beyond a binary system of "single or married"—since 2003, there's been a third option called Defacto, which refers to a category of people who live together.

New Zealand is so serious about the non-married cohabiting couple that if you have been in a "de facto" relationship for more than two years and you break up, the other person is entitled to half your assets. (Not necessarily a good thing.) Laws in the United States have not evolved to meet the changing social trend, which can cause cohabitating couples to find themselves bereft of many institutional supports. But for a number of reasons, a de facto–type policy is probably not a political reality.

Still, we could move to a more enlightened conversation about cohabitation, giving young people more education and resources about how to make a smooth and successful transition to cohabitation, and then from living together to marriage. Sassler says the takeaway from her research is that couples need to talk about situations such as the possibility of getting pregnant, whether they'll split household expenses evenly, and general expectations about gender roles.

For a more celebratory approach, Pottery Barn, Williams-Sonoma, and other stores of their ilk could even start cohabitation registries.

As for the downsides of living together, they pretty much mirror what they are for marriage. For women, more housework and more calories. (One study found that cohabiting women are more likely to gain weight.) For men, well, like with marriage, it's pretty much all upside.

SIXTEEN

Couples Should Not Live Together Before Marriage

Dan Delzell

In the following viewpoint Dan Delzell warns against living together before marriage. He bases his argument on Christian values, which preach that living together is a poor substitute for marriage, which is spiritually fulfilling. Delzell thinks living together does not indicate whether a couple will have a successful marriage. Mere cohabitation lacks the divinity, trust, and long-term commitment that are inherent in marriage. Therefore, says Delzell, it is impossible to compare the two experiences. He also says living together is a poor trial for sexual and social compatibility. Both of these things are greatly enhanced by the bounds of marriage and are likely to suffer outside of it. He concludes that people who live together and think they are getting a taste of marriage are confused about what it actually means to be married.

So you think there are advantages to living together rather than getting married. Before you close your mind any tighter on the issue, check out these five myths:

Living Together Is Not Marriage

Myth #1: Living together first will tell us if we are right for one another.

No it won't. You are comparing apples to oranges. Just because one tastes good or bad to you doesn't mean the other will taste the same. Marriage is a totally different proposition than simply living together. Marriage is built upon a promise before God to remain faithful to one another. Living together involves no such promise. You could fail at living together with someone you may have succeeded with in marriage. It all depends upon how much both people are relying on God for assistance and love. By the way, the divorce rate of couples who live together first is significantly higher than for those who do not.

If your partner will not commit to you for life, don't deceive yourself into thinking that he or she will be willing to make that commitment at some later point. Marriage is a promise to stay together. Living together for many couples lasts about 18 months, give or take. At the end of that year and a half, you still have no idea how your partner might have done if you both had taken the plunge and made a lifetime commitment to one another. Now you will never know. You settled for the easy way in and the easy way out. Your shot at true love with that person gets blown away with the wind if you decide to shack up first.

Living together prepares people to find reasons not to get married. Marriage, on the other hand, is based on unconditional love and a lifetime commitment. It is not an "audition" for marriage like you have with cohabitation. All of us are imperfect and bound to slip up at various times during the audition. Talk about conditional "love." It's "I love you" now . . . and "I will really love you" once you prove you are worthy. You better walk on eggshells in that situation. It's get pretty dicey in a hurry . . . and awkward.

Sex Outside of Marriage Has Problems

Myth #2: Living together will show us if we are sexually compatible.

No it won't. That would be true if you were animals . . . say dogs for example. You are human beings. You both have a soul. Sex between dogs is only physical. Sex between human beings was

The author believes that cohabitation is not a valid test for marital compatibility because cohabitation lacks the divinity, trust, and long-term commitment that are inherent in marriage.

designed to be physical, emotional, and spiritual. God designed it in such a way that sex outside of marriage will never produce what I would call a "spiritual orgasm." That is why it leaves you still feeling empty after the physical orgasm has gone away. Without a spiritual union through Christ, sexual compatibility is only measured in a superficial way.

If you have not yet had sex in marriage while both of you are born again and living for Christ, then you have no idea what you are missing. It is the total package . . . body, soul, and spirit. No wonder people without that union are often drawn to continue experimenting sexually to try to satisfy their hunger for a spiritual union in sex. That hunger can be satisfied, but only in marriage and only when both the husband and the wife are believers in Christ.

Marriage Is a Whole New Level of Commitment

Myth #3: We are just as committed to each other as a married couple.

No you're not. Neither of you are "all in." You are both "hedging your bets." You are both still "kicking the tires." Your "commitment" is conditional. It's not "for better or worse." Instead, it's "for better or . . . see ya, wouldn't wanna be ya." Anyone in that situation must surely feel the pressure to perform. You have been given a trial run by your partner. Aren't you lucky.

Deep down, you know in your heart that marriage is far more than a piece of paper. It is a promise before God to love and cherish your spouse for life. People who only shack up also make a promise, sort of. "I promise to do my best . . . and to watch you very closely to determine if you are worth it. If it doesn't work out . . . oh well. It's not like we were married or anything."

Living Together Without Commitment Strains Relationships

Myth #4: Our friendship won't suffer by moving in together.

That's what you think. Your friendship will soon become tense and uncomfortable. You went from courtship to "no man's land." You're not married, but you're not really dating either. How boring . . . and unnatural. No wonder the comfortable feelings of friendship soon turn into the awkward feelings that come with shacking up. It's "friends with benefits . . . minus the unconditional friendship." There is always the fear of being kicked to the curb if you don't measure up. No security. No deep peace. Hence, you end up with a strained relationship that is fraught with angst. Not exactly the ingredients of a healthy friendship.

Marriage Serves a Spiritual Purpose

Myth #5: We can love one another just as much without marriage.

No you can't. God says so. It would be true if you had evolved from a monkey. In that case, the Bible would only be a storybook filled with fantasies. As it is, you did not evolve from a monkey. You were created by God in His image. He consists of three Persons in One God . . . Father, Son, and Holy Spirit. You too are a being that is three in one . . . body, soul, and spirit. Monkeys are not three in one. God did not institute marriage between monkeys. God did not promise to bless a union of monkeys.

You have no idea how much love can fill your heart for your partner until you receive God's love in Christ and get on the "marriage train" for life. Comparing living together to marriage is comparing apples to oranges . . . and maybe even to bananas . . . you know, the kind monkeys eat.

Cohabitation Does Not Build Strong Relationships

Data compiled by the Centers for Disease Control show that men and women who lived together before marriage are more likely to end their marriages than couples who did not cohabitate prior to marriage.

What You Should Know About Dating

A 2012 study published in the journal *Psychological Science in the Public Interest* found:

- In the early 1990s fewer than 1 percent of single adult Americans dated online. By 2005, 37 percent had.
- Prior to 1978, 0.02 percent of heterosexual couples found their partners on the Web.
- Between 1979 and 1988, 0.06 percent of heterosexual couples found their partners on the Web.
- Between 1989 and 1993, 2.1 percent of heterosexual couples met online.
- Between 1994 and 1998, 3.8 percent of heterosexual couples met online.
- Between 1999 and 2003, 10.9 percent of heterosexual couples met online.
- Between 2004 and 2006, 19.3 percent of heterosexual couples met online.
- Between 2007 and 2009, 23.2 percent of heterosexual couples met online.
- By 2009, 61 percent of same-sex couples had found their partners through the Web.

A 2012 study on teen dating habits by the Robert Wood Johnson Foundation revealed:

- Seventy-five percent of students surveyed report ever having a boyfriend or girlfriend.
- More than 1 in 3 (37 percent) students surveyed report being a victim of psychological dating violence in the previous 6 months.

- Nearly 1 in 6 (15 percent) students surveyed report being a victim of physical dating violence in the previous 6 months.
- Nearly 1 in 3 (31 percent) students surveyed report being a victim of electronic dating aggression in the previous 6 months.
- More than 1 in 3 (37 percent) students surveyed report having witnessed boys or girls being physically violent to persons they were dating in the previous 6 months.
- Nearly 2 in 3 (63 percent) students surveyed strongly agree with a harmful gender stereotype, such as "girls are always trying to get boys to do what they want them to do," or "with boyfriends and girlfriends, the boy should be smarter than the girl."
- Nearly half of students (49 percent) surveyed report having been a victim of sexual harassment in the previous 6 months, such as being "touched, grabbed, or pinched in a sexual way," or that someone "made sexual jokes" about them.
- Nearly 75 percent of seventh-grade students surveyed report that, in the previous 6 months, they "sometimes or often" talk with their parents about dating topics such as "how to tell if someone might like you as a boyfriend or girlfriend."

According to Break the Cycle and the National Dating Abuse Helpline:
- About 72 percent of eighth and ninth graders are dating.
- Nearly 1.5 million high school students nationwide experience physical abuse from a dating partner in a single year.
- One in three (about 33 percent) American teens are a victim of physical, sexual, emotional, or verbal abuse from a dating partner.
- One in ten (10 percent) high school students have been purposefully hit, slapped, or physically hurt by a boyfriend or girlfriend.
- One-quarter (25 percent) of high school girls have been victims of physical or sexual abuse.

- Girls and young women between the ages of sixteen and twenty-four experience the highest rate of intimate partner violence—almost triple the national average.
- Violent behavior typically begins between the ages of twelve and eighteen.
- Teen girls who are physically or sexually abused are six times more likely to become pregnant and twice as likely to get a sexually transmitted infection.
- Half of youth who have been victims of both dating violence and rape attempt suicide, compared to 12.5 percent of nonabused girls and 5.4 percent of nonabused boys.
- Eight states do not include dating relationships in their definition of domestic violence. As a result, young victims of dating abuse often cannot apply for restraining orders.
- New Hampshire is the only state where the law specifically allows a minor of any age to apply for a protection order; more than half of states do not specify the minimum age of a petitioner.
- Currently only one juvenile domestic violence court in the country focuses exclusively on teen dating violence.
- Only 33 percent of teens who were in a violent relationship ever told anyone about the abuse.
- Eighty-one percent of parents either believe teen dating violence is not an issue or say they are unsure if it is an issue.

In 2010 the BBC World Service polled 10,976 Internet users across nineteen countries and found:
- Almost one in three (30 percent) Web users regard the Internet as a good place to find a boyfriend or girlfriend.
- Among Internet users, men are somewhat more enthusiastic about finding a partner online than women—33 percent of men regard the Internet as a good place to find a boyfriend or girlfriend, versus 27 percent of women.
- Thirty-six percent of respondents aged eighteen to twenty-four said the Internet is a good place to find a boyfriend or girlfriend.

- Twenty-three percent of respondents sixty-five and older said the Internet is a good place to find a boyfriend or girlfriend.
- Twenty-eight percent of those with a university education felt the Internet is a good place to find a partner.
- Thirty-six percent of those who had not completed high school felt the Internet is a good place to find a partner.
- The country where the most people agreed the Internet is a good place to find a partner is Pakistan, where 60 percent said the Internet is a good place to find a partner.
- In India 59 percent said the Internet is a good place to find a partner.
- In Ghana 47 percent said the Internet is a good place to find a partner.
- In the Philippines 42 percent said the Internet is a good place to find a partner.
- In the United Kingdom 28 percent said the Internet is a good place to find a partner.
- In France 27 percent said the Internet is a good place to find a partner.
- In the United States 21 percent said the Internet is a good place to find a partner.
- In South Korea 16 percent said the Internet is a good place to find a partner.

According to *Online Dating Magazine*:
- Five percent of Internet users have paid to use an online dating service.
- Seventeen percent of couples who were married in the past three years met on an online dating service.
- One out of every five singles in the United States have dated someone they met online.
- Online dating is the third most popular way for singles to meet, behind school/work and friend/family member.

What You Should Do About Dating

For most teens a first relationship is built on stolen kisses, tender confessions, and a feeling of belonging and acceptance during an otherwise insecure and confusing time of life. But for some, high school relationships are marked by cruel and manipulative put-downs, emotional battering, physical violence, and sexual pressuring or rape, the scars of which can last a lifetime.

Though teen dating violence is a problem that most adults either do not know about or do not believe exists, about one in eleven teens reports experiencing some form of it in their relationship. The Centers for Disease Control and Prevention reports that more than half of all US teens are in a romantic relationship; this means that millions of young people in the United States are engaging in the joys of dating, but also its pressures. In fact, 1.5 million teens report being victimized by their partner. Understanding what constitutes dating violence is an important part of preventing it.

Recognizing Dating Violence

Dating violence takes many forms, some easier to recognize than others. Physical violence is fairly straightforward, though devastating to deal with. According to the Centers for Disease Control and Prevention, 9.4 percent of high school students report being hit, slapped, or physically hurt on purpose by their boyfriend or girlfriend in the previous year. Other forms of physical violence include grabbing, shoving, choking, kicking, or otherwise touching someone in a way that causes pain or is unwelcome. It is never OK to hurt someone or for someone else to hurt you in this way—no matter what.

Other forms of dating violence are more subtle, which means that in addition to being abused, a victim may not even be sure abuse is occurring. In fact, telling a person "you are crazy" or the person's fears of abuse are "all in your head" is a form of this insidious type of abuse. Other examples of emotional, verbal, or psychological dating violence include when a partner makes snide, hurtful, calculating comments under the guise of "just joking"; when a partner reacts overly harshly to a mistake or punishes the erring partner disproportionately to the mistake; when a partner cruelly withholds affection; when a partner is controlling or unnecessarily jealous; and when a partner twists information or tries to distort a victim's memory and perception of the situation (a type of psychological abuse called "gaslighting"). Sexual abuse, too, can be tricky to identify; it is often unclear whether one person is unfairly pressuring the other or otherwise trapping the other person into a sexual situation that is unwelcome or for which the other person is unprepared. The ambiguity of these situations is only compounded when alcohol and drugs are added to the mix. Surveys by Teenage Research Unlimited reveal that 25 percent of teenage girls have been pressured to perform sexual acts, while 26 percent of teenage girls have been verbally abused.

One student at Nevada Union High School shared her story of a relationship that featured this type of abuse. Like many relationships, she and her boyfriend started out strong; she could not wait to see or hear from him, and he made her feel special, beautiful, and loved. But over time, his controlling behavior isolated her from friends and family:

> As time went by, I could just feel the cage walls closing in, the door shutting and hearing the "click" of a lock in my head. I lost all my friends, privacy, and so much more. I wasn't allowed to talk to anyone, not even my girlfriends I had for 11 years. My phone was checked to make sure I wasn't talking to anyone but him and that no one was trying to talk to me. My Facebook page was deactivated as well as my e-mail.

> Everyday I had to tell him where I was on campus, and what class I was leaving or going to. . . . When I tried to leave he knew how to pull me back in. I felt like I was just a chess piece

in his mental game. I couldn't tell anyone and tried not to show it but it was difficult.[1]

"Amanda" recounts a similar tale of abuse that featured emotional manipulation, control, jealousy, and isolation:

I had to call him in the morning before I left for school and during my lunch period. After school, if I hung out with my friends in the parking lot instead of leaving school immediately to go to his place, he would question who I was with and what I was doing. Then, the accusations started. He claimed that I was cheating on him, seeing someone else behind his back. I didn't know how this was possible, seeing as how I was with him every waking moment that I wasn't at school or working (and we just happened to work together). I tried to defend myself, but he would just get angry and scream at me. He told me not to even bother breaking up with him, because no one would want me, and I would end up all alone again with no one to love me. Once again, he played on my vulnerabilities, because all I wanted was to be loved.[2]

Talk to Someone or Be an Ear for a Friend

When asked by a research company what they would do if they found themselves in an abusive relationship, nearly 3 in 4 teens said they would turn to a friend for help. Yet in reality, only about 1 in 3 teens who suffer dating abuse in a relationship tell anyone about what is really going on. Less than 1 in 4 discuss the problem with their parents, and more than 3 in 4 stay in the relationship.

Sharing your reality, no matter how awful or embarrassing, is the first step to changing it. But many teens do not talk to anyone for fear of reprisal from their partner, getting in trouble with their parents, or being judged by their friends. It is important to work through these barriers to get help, because abusive situations rarely resolve themselves, and they typically get worse.

If there is absolutely no one in your immediate circle you can talk to, you will find support at the National Teen Dating Abuse

(NTDA) Helpline. They have thousands of peer advocates (that is, teens and young adults who have experience with dating issues) on hand to offer advice, refer you to support services in your area, discuss with you potential legal or law enforcement solutions, or just listen. All conversations are free, anonymous, and private. All you might need to tell the person is your first name and your general location (nearest city) so they can put you in touch with appropriate local resources.

There are a lot of ways to get in touch with this organization. You can call them toll-free, twenty-four hours a day, at (866) 331-9474. The peer advocate you will talk to is trained to discuss all of the embarrassing, painful, shameful, infuriating, or otherwise sensitive issues you are likely to bring up. They are also ready to conduct conversations with concerned friends, family members, teachers, and other people who can call on behalf of someone in an abusive relationship.

If a phone call is too difficult to manage, the NTDA Helpline also runs a useful texting service. Texting "loveis" to 77054 will put you in touch with a peer advocate who can respond to a question and send you a link to a resource or service that you can access from your phone. The NTDA Helpline does not charge for this service, but texting fees apply as per your service agreement. The NTDA recommends that victims who use this service delete the texts from their phone after they send and receive information.

If your situation or question is too large for a text message, you can live chat with a peer advocate. The NTDA Helpline's website offers an instant-message feature in which you can connect with a support person in real time. The chat feature is not a public chat room and is not affiliated with a general chat messenger service (such as iChat, GChat, or Yahoo Chat). Rather, it is a private, one-on-one session with the same advocates who run the toll-free helpline. You can access the chat feature at www.loveisrespect.org.

What Should I Say?

Whether contacting the NTDA Helpline or speaking with a trusted family member, friend, teacher, or other figure, it will likely be difficult for you to know where to begin. If you need some help getting started, you can use the following prompts and questions:

- I need to share something that has been going on with me.
- Can you be the person I trust with a difficult situation?
- I am unhappy and do not know what to do.
- Can you tell me if the following behavior/comment/dynamic sounds like it is abusive?
- Something happened recently and I am not sure how to feel about it.

Or, if you are concerned that someone in your life is experiencing abuse, you can try broaching a conversation with him or her using one of the following questions or statements:

- You seem different lately. Is something going on that you want to talk about?
- I just wanted to let you know you can share things with me, and I will not judge you.
- I was reading about relationship abuse and it made me worry for you.
- I thought maybe if you had an outside perspective on the matter, it might help you see your situation more clearly.
- Can you lay out for me what has been going on, and we can work through it together?

No matter how you begin a conversation, know that initiating it is often the most difficult part. Once you start talking, you will likely be amazed by what comes out, and also how good it feels no longer to be alone with your secret.

Notes

1. Quoted in Domestic Violence and Sexual Assault Coalition, "Teen Dating Stories," February 2012. www.dvsac.org/anony mous-teen-nevada-union-high-school- february-2012.
2. Amanda, "Love Hurts: A Story of Teenage Abuse," Yahoo!, January 29, 2007. http://voices.yahoo.com/love-hurts-story-teenage-abuse-175566.html.

ORGANIZATIONS TO CONTACT

The editors have compiled the following list of organizations concerned with the issues debated in this book. The descriptions are derived from materials provided by the organizations. All have publications or information available for interested readers. The list was compiled on the date of publication of the present volume; names, addresses, phone and fax numbers, and e-mail and Internet addresses may change. Be aware that many organizations take several weeks or longer to respond to inquiries, so allow as much time as possible.

Abstinence & Marriage Education Partnership (A&M)
411 Business Center Dr., Ste. 103
Mt. Prospect, IL 60056
(877) 290-9248
website: www.ampartnership.org

The goal of this organization is to send every teenager in the country the message of abstinence and marriage. A&M has developed a series of curricula for teenagers and offers these materials to pregnancy centers, public and private schools, churches, and community organizations throughout the country. Among its publications pertaining to teen dating are "Marriage First Then a Baby" and "Personal Responsibility as a Matter of Honor."

Advocates for Youth
2000 M St. NW, Ste. 750
Washington, DC 20036
(202) 419-3420
website: www.advocatesforyouth.org

Established in 1980 as the Center for Population Options, Advocates for Youth champions efforts that help young people make informed and responsible decisions about their reproductive and sexual health. Pamphlets, articles, and outreach services address a variety of issues that intersect with teen dating, relationships, and sexual activity.

Child Trends
4301 Connecticut Ave. NW, Ste. 350
Washington, DC 20008
(202) 572-6000
website: www.childtrends.org

Child Trends works to analyze contraceptive use among teens and uses statistics and research to educate the teenage population to become consistent users of contraception. The organization produces many publications, including, "Facts at a Glance," which incorporates city, state, and national statistics on teen pregnancy, childbearing, sexuality, and other issues that result from teen dating.

Coalition for Positive Sexuality (CPS)
PO Box 77212
Washington, DC 20013
(773) 604-1654
website: www.positive.org

The CPS is a grassroots direct-action group formed in the spring of 1992 by high school students and activists. The coalition works to counteract the institutionalized misogyny, heterosexism, homophobia, racism, and ageism that students experience every day at school. It is dedicated to offering teens sexuality and safe-sex education that is pro-woman, pro–lesbian/gay/bisexual, pro–safe sex, and pro-choice. Its motto is "Have fun and be safe." The CPS publishes the pamphlet *Just Say Yes*, which refers to saying yes to safe, appropriate, and welcomed sexual experiences and no to unwanted, unsafe, or irresponsible sexual experiences.

Crisis Intervention Center
5603 S. Fourteenth St.
Fort Smith, AR 72901
(479) 782-1821
hotline: (800) 359-0056
website: www.crisisinterventioncenter.org

The mission statement of Crisis Intervention Center is to end domestic violence and sexual assault among people of all ages. Recognizing that sexting has resulted in sexual assault, bullying, and suicide, the center offers information and fact sheets related to sexting, sex, and other issues that come into play in teenage relationships; it also offers a hotline teens can call should they feel overwhelmed by problems resulting from these issues.

Family Research Council (FRC)
801 G St. NW
Washington, DC 20001
(202) 393-2100
e-mail: corrdept@frc.org
website: www.frc.org

The FRC is a research, resource, and education organization that promotes the traditional family. It opposes condom distribution programs in schools and encourages teens that are in relationships to abstain from sexual activity. Among the council's numerous publications are the papers "Revolt of the Virgins," "Abstinence: The New Sexual Revolution," "Abstinence Programs Show Promise in Reducing Sexual Activity and Pregnancy Among Teens," and "Adolescent Health and Sexuality: Research Findings."

Focus on the Family
8605 Explorer Dr.
Colorado Springs, CO 80995
(719) 531-5181
website: www.fotf.org

This organization promotes Christian values and strong family ties. It campaigns for abstinence until marriage and encourages teens in relationships to be chaste. It publishes the monthly magazine *Focus on the Family* and sells many books on its website that promote abstinence, such as *Wait for Me: Rediscovering the Purity of Joy in Romance*. Among its numerous publications are "Risk Factors for Premarital Sex" and "How Sex Impacts Teen Girls."

Guttmacher Institute
125 Maiden Ln.
New York, NY 10038
(212) 248-1111
e-mail: info@guttmacher.org
website: www.guttmacher.org

Considered an authoritative and trustworthy source of data by both liberals and conservatives, the Guttmacher Institute works to protect and expand the reproductive choices of all women and men. It strives to ensure that people have access to the information and services they need to exercise their rights and responsibilities concerning sexual activity, reproduction, and family planning. It publishes a wealth of data and information on teen pregnancy, sex education programs, teen contraception use, and other subjects that will be useful for students seeking information about issues regarding teen dating. An entire section of the institute's website is devoted to adolescents (www.guttmacher.org/sections/adolescents.php).

Healthy Teen Network
1501 St. Paul St., Ste. 124
Baltimore, MD 21202
(410) 685-0481
website: www.healthyteennetwork.org

Healthy Teen Network is a national organization that focuses on adolescent health issues, including teen dating, teen sex, and teen pregnancy. It is a network of health specialists, therapists, and reproductive health care professionals who support sexual health for teens at the city, state, and federal level. It publishes many publications, including *Helping Teens Stay Healthy and Safe: Birth Control and Confidential Services* and *A Tool to Assess the Characteristics of Effective Sex and STD/HIV Education Programs.*

Heritage Foundation
214 Massachusetts Ave. NE
Washington, DC 20002

(202) 546-4400
e-mail: info@heritage.org
website: www.heritage.org

The Heritage Foundation is a public policy research institute that believes the welfare system has contributed to the problems of illegitimacy and teenage pregnancy. Some of the foundation's numerous publications include "Abstinence Education: Assessing the Evidence," "Adolescent Virginity Pledges, Condom Use, and Sexually Transmitted Diseases Among Young Adults," and "Adolescent Virginity Pledges and Risky Sexual Behaviors."

Kaiser Family Foundation
1330 G St. NW
Washington, DC 20005
(202) 347-5270
fax: (202) 347-5274
website: www.kff.org

The Kaiser Family Foundation is a nonprofit research organization focusing on health care issues, including those related to teen dating issues. Among its numerous publications that relate to teen sexual heath is SexSmarts, a survey of teens about virginity. Other publications consider the role of technology in teens' sexual lives.

National Campaign to Prevent Teen Pregnancy
1176 Massachusetts Ave. NW
Washington, DC 20036
(202) 478-8500
website: www.teenpregnancy.org

The mission of the National Campaign to Prevent Teen Pregnancy is to reduce teenage and unplanned pregnancy by promoting a combination of abstinence and contraception education for adolescents. The campaign publishes pamphlets, brochures, and opinion polls that include *Not Yet: Programs to Delay First Sex Among Teens*; *The Next Best Thing: Helping Sexually Active*

Teens Avoid Pregnancy; and *What Helps in Providing Contraceptive Services to Teens?* The campaign also sponsors numerous websites, such as StayTeen.org, that address issues and questions pertaining to teen dating.

Planned Parenthood Federation of America
434 W. Thirty-Third St.
New York, NY 10011
(212) 541-7800
e-mail: communications@ppfa.org
website: www.plannedparenthood.org

The Planned Parenthood Federation of America believes individuals have the right to control their own fertility without government interference. It promotes comprehensive sex education and provides contraceptive counseling and services through clinics across the United States. Its publications include the brochures *Guide to Birth Control: Seven Accepted Methods of Contraception*; *Teen Sex? It's Okay to Say No Way*; and the bimonthly newsletter *LinkLine*.

Religious Coalition for Reproductive Choice
1413 K St. NW, 14th Fl.
Washington, DC 20005
(202) 628-770
e-mail: info@rcrc.org
website: www.rcrc.org

The coalition works to inform the media and the public that many mainstream religions support reproductive options, including birth control. It works to make birth control affordable to America's poorest citizens and supports the Prevention Through Affordable Access Act as well as the Responsible Education About Life Act. The coalition also publishes numerous articles pertaining to issues relating to teen dating, including "The Role of Religious Congregations in Fostering Adolescent Sexual Health."

**Sexuality Information and Education Council
of the United States (SIECUS)**
90 John St., Ste. 704
New York, NY 10038
(212) 819-9770
e-mail: pmalone@siecus.org
website: www.siecus.org

SIECUS is an organization of educators, physicians, social workers, and others who support the individual's right to acquire knowledge of sexuality and who encourage responsible sexual behavior. The council promotes comprehensive sex education for all children that includes AIDS education, teaching about homosexuality, and instruction about contraceptives and sexually transmitted diseases. Its publications include fact sheets, annotated bibliographies by topic, the booklet *Talk About Sex*, and the monthly *SIECUS Report*.

BIBLIOGRAPHY

Books

Kathleen A. Bogle, *Hooking Up: Sex, Dating, and Relationships on Campus*. New York: New York University Press, 2008.

Donna Freitas, *The End of Sex: How Hookup Culture Is Leaving a Generation Unhappy, Sexually Unfulfilled, and Confused About Intimacy*. New York: Basic, 2013.

Miriam Grossman, *Unprotected: A Campus Psychiatrist Reveals How Political Correctness in Her Profession Endangers Every Student*. New York: Sentinel Trade, 2007.

Joe S. McIlhaney, Freda McKissic Bush, and Stan Guthrie, *Girls Uncovered: New Research on What America's Sexual Culture Does to Young Women*. Chicago, IL: Moody, 2011.

Hanna Rosin, *The End of Men: And the Rise of Women*. New York: Riverhead, 2012.

Rachel Simmons, *The Curse of the Good Girl: Raising Authentic Girls with Courage and Confidence*. New York: Penguin, 2009.

Jessica Valenti, *The Purity Myth: How America's Obsession with Virginity Is Hurting Young Women*. Berkeley, CA: Seal, 2009.

Periodicals and Internet Sources

Associated Press, "Cohabitation Before Marriage? It's No Greater Divorce Risk," *Christian Science Monitor*, March 22, 2012. www.csmonitor.com/The-Culture/Family/2012/0322/Cohabitation-before-marriage-It-s-no-greater-divorce-risk.

Sandy Banks, "Black Woman, White Man: Should Race Matter in Love?," *Los Angeles Times*, October 7, 2011. http://articles.latimes.com/2011/oct/07/local/la-me-1008-banks-20111008.

William J. Bennett, "Hookup Culture Debases Women," CNN, April 4, 2012. www.cnn.com/2012/04/04/opinion/bennett-modern-women/index.html.

Carl Bialik, "How Many Marriages Started with Online-Dating Sites?," *WJS Blogs, Wall Street Journal*, July 28, 2009. http://blogs.wsj.com/numbersguy/how-many-marriages-started-online-764.

Carl Bialik, "Marriage-Maker Claims Are Tied in Knots: Online Dating Sites Say Hordes of People Ultimately Marry, but Their Methods Have Plenty of Hitches of Their Own," *Wall Street Journal*, July 29, 2009. http://online.wsj.com/article/SB124879877347487253.html.

Charles M. Blow, "The Demise of Dating," *New York Times*, December 13, 2008. www.nytimes.com/2008/12/13/opinion/13blow.html.

Johannah Cornblatt, "How Match.com Changed Dating," *Newsweek*, August 31, 2010. www.thedailybeast.com/newsweek/2010/08/31/how-match-com-changed-online-dating.html.

Suzanne D'Amato, "Modern Romance: Hook-Up Culture," *Teen Vogue*, May 2009. www.teenvogue.com/advice/2009-05/teens-talk-about-sex-and-hooking-up.

Tina deVaron, "At Colleges Plagued with Date Rape, Why 'No' Still Means 'Yes,'" *Christian Science Monitor*, June 28, 2011. www.csmonitor.com/Commentary/Opinion/2011/0628/At-colleges-plagued-with-date-rape-why-no-still-means-yes.

Amy Dudley, "Together We Must End Dating Violence," *1 Is 2 Many* (blog), White House, December 27, 2012. www.whitehouse.gov/blog/2012/02/27/together-we-must-end-dating-violence.

Abby Ellin, "The Recession. Isn't It Romantic?," *New York Times*, February 12, 2009. www.nytimes.com/2009/02/12/fashion/12dating.html.

Daniel Elliot, "Online Dating Is Social Suicide," *Tomatalk* (Kamiakin High School, Kennewick, WA) February 7, 2012. www.tomatalk.com/opinion/2012/02/07/online-dating-is-social-suicide.

Eli J. Finkel and Benjamin R. Karney, "Online Dating Sites Don't Match Hype," *New York Times*, February 2, 2012. www.nytimes

.com/2012/02/12/opinion/sunday/online-dating-sites-dont
-match-hype.html.

Caitlin Flanagan, "Love, Actually," *Atlantic*, June 2010. www
.theatlantic.com/magazine/archive/2010/06/love-actually
/308094/1/?single page=true.

Sarah Foster, "Despite Parents' Opinion, Couples Should Live
Together Before Marriage," OnMilwaukee.com, November 20,
2010. http://onmilwaukee.com/living/articles/livingtogether
.html.

Katy Grimes, "Not Another Teen Regulation Bill," *CalWatchdog*,
February 22, 2012. www.calwatchdog.com/2012/02/22/not
-another-teen-regulation-bill.

Pierce Harlan and E. Steven Berkimer (False Rape Society),
"Spinning Our Wheels on 'Date Rape': Time for a New
Approach," Voice for Men, February 12, 2011. www.avoicefor
men.com/mens-rights/false-rape-culture/spinning-our-wheels
-on-date-rape-time-for-a-new-approach.

Meg Jay, "The Downside of Cohabitating Before Marriage," *New
York Times*, April 14, 2012. www.nytimes.com/2012/04/15
/opinion/sunday/the-downside-of-cohabiting-before-marriage
.html?pagewanted=all.

Sharon Jayson, "More College 'Hookups,' but More Virgins, Too,"
USA Today, March 30, 2011. www.usatoday.com/news/health
/wellness/dating/story/2011/03/More-hookups-on-campuses-but
-more-virgins-too/45556388/1.

Stuart Jeffries, "Is Online Dating Destroying Love?," *Guardian*
(London), February 6, 2012. www.guardian.co.uk/lifeand
style/2012/feb/06/is-online-dating-destroying-love.

Porter Kaplan, "Why I Use a Dating Spreadsheet," *New York Daily
News*, April 22, 2012. http://articles.nydailynews.com/2012-04
-22/news/31383993_1_spreadsheet-potential-date-track.

Jenna Kern-Rugile, "Early Dating's Perils for Kids," *Newsday*, April
5, 2012. www.newsday.com/opinion/oped/kern-rugile-early
-dating-s-perils-for-kids-1.3645330.

David Lazarus, "Accountability Is Overdue on Dating Websites," *Los Angeles Times*, March 23, 2012. http://articles.latimes .com/2012/mar/23/business/la-fi-lazarus-20120323.

Shan Li, "Smartphone Dating Apps Link Users by Proximity," *Los Angeles Times*, May 18, 2011. http://articles.latimes.com/2011 /may/18/business/la-fi-dating-apps-20110518.

Alexis Madrigal, "Take the Data out of Dating," *Atlantic*, December 2010. www.theatlantic.com/magazine/archive/2010/12/take-the -data-out-of-dating/8299.

Mike Males and Anthony Bernier, "Teen Dating Violence: The Invented Epidemic," YouthFacts, August 28, 2008. www.youth facts.org/tndatvio.php.

Amanda Marcotte, "It's Not the Sex, It's the Sexism," *Raw Story*, February 28, 2010. www.rawstory.com/rs/2010/02/28/pandagon -its_not_the_sex_its_the_sexism.

Merced (CA) Sun Star, "Teacher-Pupil Dating Law Needed," April 3, 2012. www.mercedsunstar.com/2012/04/03/2294255/our -view-teacher-pupil-dating.html.

Carole Mikita, "Utah Teens Share Stories of Dating Violence," *Deseret News* (Salt Lake City, UT), February 14, 2011. www .deseretnews.com/article/705366692/Utah-teens-share-stories -of-dating-violence.html?pg=all.

Maura Pennington, "The Economics of Post-collegiate Dating," *Forbes*, December 20, 2011. www.forbes.com/sites/maurapen nington/2011/12/20/the-economics-of-post-collegiate-dating.

Andrea Peyser, "Where You @, Romeo," *New York Post*, April 23, 2012. www.nypost.com/p/news/local/where_you_romeo _YUu93CPNsskP6rWg1oXjqK.

Irene Rochel Pritsker, "The Case for Religious Dating in a Modern World," CrownHeights.info, January 4, 2011. www.crown heights.info/index.php?itemid=31330.

Amanda Robb, "How Online Dating Really Works—Why You'll Never Find Love Online," *Marie Claire*, August 16, 2010. www .marieclaire.com/sex-love/relationship-issues/how-online-dat ing-really-works.

Stephanie Rosenbloom, "No Scrolling Required at New Dating Sites," *New York Times*, April 15, 2012. www.nytimes.com /2012/04/15/fashion/no-scrolling-required-at-new-dating-sites .html?pagewanted=all.

Hanna Rosin, "Boys on the Side," *Atlantic*, September 2012. www.theatlantic.com/magazine/archive/2012/09/boys-on-the -side/309062.

Hanna Rosin, "The End of Men," *Atlantic*, July/August 2012. www.theatlantic.com/magazine/archive/2010/07/the-end-of -men/308135.

Sherry Schultz, "The Trauma and Scars of Date Rape," *Milwaukee Journal Sentinel*, February 25, 2012. www.json line.com/news/opinion/the-trauma-and-scars-of-date-rape -1m41j5b-140383793.html.

Rachel Simmons, "Is Hooking Up Good for Girls?" Rachel Simmons.com, February 25, 2010. www.rachelsimmons.com /2010/02/why-the-hook-up-culture-is-hurting-girls.

Andrew Stern, "Researchers Say Dating Websites Make Poor Cupids," *Columbus (OH) Dispatch*, February 7, 2012. www .dispatch.com/content/stories/national_world/2012/02/07 /researchers-say-dating-websites-make-poor-cupids.html.

John Tilley, "Extend Violence Protection to Dating Couples," *Lexington (KY) Herald Leader*, March 18, 2012. www.kentucky .com/2012/03/18/2115993/ky-voices-extend-violence-protec tion.html.

John Wildermuth, "Surprise, Surprise, 18-Year-Olds Are Adults," Fox&Hounds, April 27, 2012. www.foxandhoundsdaily .com/2012/04/surprise-surprise-18-year-olds-are-adults.

Jenna Wortham, "In Online Dating, Taking a Chance on Love and Algorithms," *New York Times*, April 7, 2012. www.nytimes .com/2012/04/08/technology/in-online-dating-taking-a-chance -on-love-and-algorithms.html.

Websites

Love Is Respect (www.lovisrespect.org). Featuring numerous articles, blog entries, and videos, this site helps teens prevent dating violence and cell phone and social media harassment, and it pushes the message that true love features respect.

Safe Teens (www.safeteens.org). Sponsored by the Pennsylvania Department of Health, this site features advice for teens grappling with issues related to relationships, sex, pregnancy, and other subjects.

Stay Teen (www.stayteen.org). This site, sponsored by the National Campaign to Prevent Teen Pregnancy, offers loads of dating advice for teens, including how to say no to sex before you are ready and what constitutes appropriate relationship behaviors, actions, and language. It also features posts and questions from real readers.

T.E.A.R.—Teens Experiencing Abusive Relationships (www .teensagainstabuse.org). This site offers a place where teens in an abusive relationship can turn for help, advice, and support. The website defines dating violence, explains who is at risk, and offers numerous resources for support.

Teen Dating Violence Awareness Month (http://teendvmonth .org). This site, sponsored by the organization Break the Cycle, focuses on how to prevent teen dating violence.

A Thin Line (www.athinline.org). This site represents an MTV campaign against sexting, cyberbullying, and digital dating abuse. It contains inspirational stories from celebrities and advice regarding sexting and other digital issues.

INDEX

Foley, Aaron, 50

G
Gavin, Jeff, 35
Girls Uncovered (McIlhaney and Bush), 19, 23
Girls/women
advances made by, 19
chastity empowers, 23
messages media sends to, 26–28, 29
must value own desires, 29–31
Glamour (magazine), 28

H
Hamby, Sherry L., 54, 55
Hammond, Robert, 36
Harding, Kate, 24
Harper, Charlotte, 35
Hooker, James, *77*, 78
Hooking up/hook-up culture, 5–8
is not sexist, 24–31
is sexist, 18–23
perception of college students on prevalence of, *12*
preference for, by gender, *21*
pros/cons of, 13

J
Jay, Meg, 86
Journal of Adolescent Research, 11

K
Karney, Benjamin, 43
Kling, Rebecca, 81

M
Mac Donald, Heather, 70
Markoff, Philip H., *52*, 52–53
Marriage
cohabitation *vs.*, 92
commitment and, 94
percentage of young people cohabiting before, 89
as serving spiritual purpose, 94–95
sexuality free from, harms women, 19–20
Match.com (online dating site), 35
McDonnell, Meg, 14
McIlhaney, Joe, 19
Miller, Amanda, 87–88, 89
Montoya, Matthew, 46

N
National Marriage Project (University of Virginia), 16

O
Office of Civil Rights (US Department of Justice), 72
Olsen, Kristin, 77, 78, 80
Opinion polls. *See* Surveys